50 Shades of Stitches

Contemporary Openwork

Knitting Patterns
with Step-by-Step Instructions and
Author's Methods of How to Make Perfect Double
Yarn Over and Knit 2 Together More Evenly

Marina Molo

Printed in the United States of America First Printing, 2020
ISBN **978-1-63227-324-6**

SCR MEDIA Inc
Box 7103
Delray Beach Fl 33482
561-909-6975

If you like this book and found some benefit in reading it, I'd like to hear from you and hope that you could take some time to post a review on Amazon. Your feedback and support will help the author to greatly improve her writing craft for future projects and make this book even better. Just type this link into your web browser Getbook.at/Vol5 or scan QR code.

Praise

"Add new life to your library with this fabulous stitch dictionary from designer Marina Molo. It's packed with great patterns, utilizing cables and lace stitches and more for wonderful textured effects."

Simply Knitting Magazine

"Amazing stitches with very detailed instructions. Would recommend to knitters of all levels"

Goodreads.com

"I began 50 Shades of Stitches with my intention being only reading; however, the interesting patterns made me want to try them out and even share them with family and friends. Marina Molo's skills and experience in teaching knitting becomes evident immediately; she has delivered a quality product in 50 Shades of Stitches that anyone interested in knitting will benefit from. Whether for hats or scarves, sweaters or more, 50 Shades of Stitches will be an excellent guide for unique and quality patterns."

Readers Favorite

"Has some really nice patterns I have never seen before."

Nina's At My House

"With Marina Molo's knitting expertise at your fingertips, you have all the tools you need to create patterns that finally make your dreamdesigns a reality. This timeless and influential book is poised toinspire a whole new generation of knitters who have yet to discover the joys and comforts of knitting."

Unraveling Podcast

Contents

Pattern 1

Pattern 2

Pattern 3

Pattern 4

Pattern 5

Pattern 6

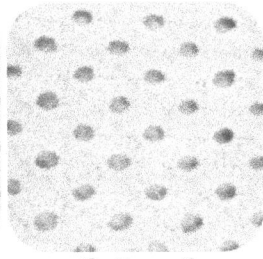
Pattern 7

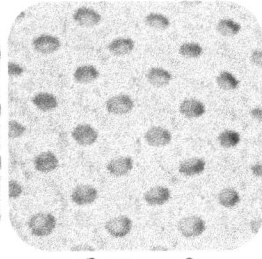
Pattern 8

Pattern 9

Pattern 10

Pattern 11

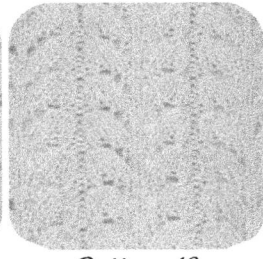
Pattern 12

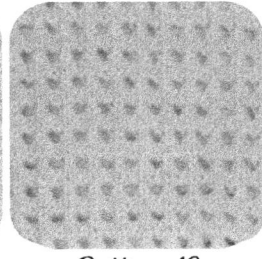
Pattern 13

Pattern 14

Pattern 15

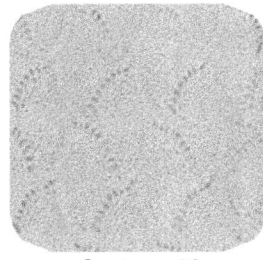
Pattern 16

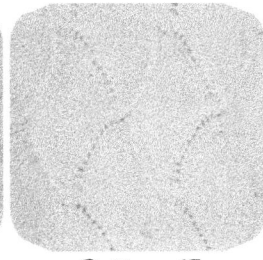
Pattern 17

Pattern 18

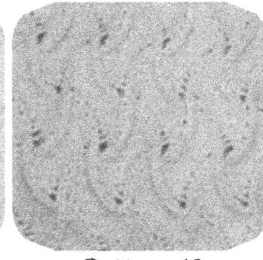
Pattern 19

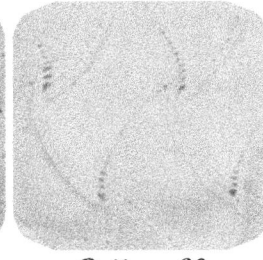
Pattern 20

Pattern 21

Pattern 22

Pattern 23

Pattern 24

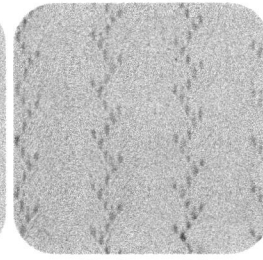
Pattern 25

Pattern 26

Pattern 27

Pattern 28

Pattern 29

Pattern 30

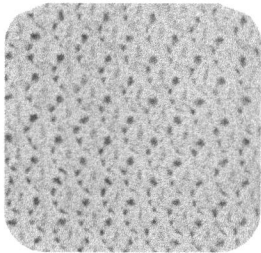

Pattern 31

Pattern 32

Pattern 33

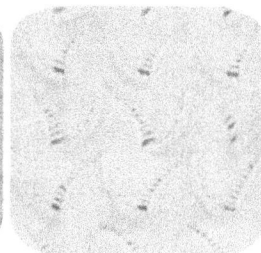

Pattern 34

Pattern 35

Pattern 36

Pattern 37

Pattern 38

Pattern 39

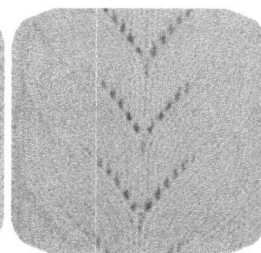

Pattern 40

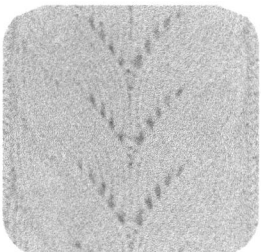

Pattern 41

Pattern 42

Pattern 43

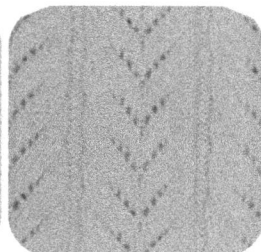

Pattern 44

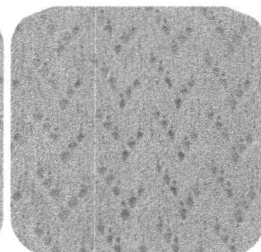

Pattern 45

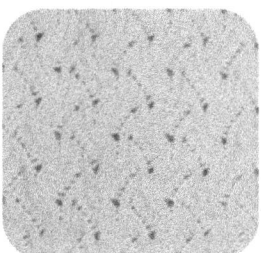

Pattern 46

Pattern 47

Pattern 48

Pattern 49

Pattern 50

Introduction

All openwork patterns have the same knitting principle, consisting of working 2 stitches together and making a yarn over to compensate for a missing stitch. Thus appear simple openwork patterns and seemingly complicated endless myriads of whimsical ornaments that we all like.

Despite the simplicity of the openwork technique, many knitters consider it complicated, as such patterns often require more time for knitting and more concentration on the process during the work. Openwork stitches are also challenging to knit evenly because of frequently knitted 2 stitches together and endless yarn overs. Uneven stitches are especially noticeable in chains of knitted 2 stockinet stitches together, with a slant to the right or left. Regardless of how hard you try, stubborn stitches refuse to come out even, and many knitters avoid openwork patterns for this reason alone. This book shows how to improve the evenness of openwork stitches and significantly heighten the quality of knits.

As you know, stitches can be worked through the front legs or the back legs. When openwork patterns are knitted through the back legs, the stitches come out more tightly and, therefore, more even, whereas knitting through the front legs makes them more loose and stretchable. However, in some openwork patterns, especially with frequently knitted 2 stitches together, knitting through the back legs may not shrink the stitches' size. In such cases, can be used method of twisted stitches, which can reduce their size.

Twisted stitch is a particular method of knitting. These stitches, as regular ones, can also be knitted two ways. The first way is based on knitting through the front legs, and the second way is based on knitting through the back legs. The same as regular stitches, twisted stitches knitted through the back legs come out tighter than stitches knitted through the front legs. Twisted stitches are frequently used in openwork patterns to increase the tightness of too loose stitches when otherwise it is impossible. Twisted stitches are smaller and tighter than regular ones and look like tiny braids. For some patterns, they are essential; for others, their use is optional. Let's look at both ways of knitting.

In the first way, based on regular knitting through the front legs, the knit stitch works through the back leg, instead of the front leg as usual, and the purl stitch works through the back leg too, instead of the front leg as usual; however, the purl stitch works the same way as in regular knitting through the front leg, setting up the knit stitch for knitting through the front leg; thus, the stitch becomes twisted.

In a second way, in twisted stitches based on regular knitting through the back legs, the front leg moves to the back, and then this stitch works through the back leg. The purl stitch works through the back leg, too, instead of the front leg, as usual, as in regular knitting through the back leg, setting up the knit stitch for knitting through the back leg; stitch becomes twisted.

There are particular ways of working edge stitches to avoid stretched edges. There are several, but the most frequently used are the following three. In the first, regardless of the way of knitting, through the front legs or the back legs, the first edge stitch slips onto the right needle, and the last edge stitch purls as in knitting through the back leg (see recommendations below). This way, the last edge stitch comes out tighter than purling it otherwise, i.e., as in knitting through the front leg (see recommendations below).

In the second way of knitting edge stitches, both the first and the last edge stitches knit through the front leg. In the third way, the first edge stitch slips onto the right needle, inserting the right needle through the front leg from left to right, and the last edge stitch knits through the front leg. The last two methods create tight and even edges, which do not curl up and hold the shape well. These methods suit well for patterns in which, otherwise, the edges come out uneven, with the stretched left side. The third method creates even knotted edges, which are especially suitable for scarves.

There are also methods of improving the evenness of openwork patterns in general. Especially, knitted 2 stockinet stitches together, with a slant to the left or right, which often come out uneven. For instance, using thinner needles than recommended can reduce the size of stitches and make them tighter and more even. Controlling yarn tension can also make stitches tighter, and, therefore, smaller and more even. Twisting the 2nd stitch behind the 1st one clockwise twice allows receiving evenly knitted 2 stitches together, with a slant to the left or to the right, as the twisted 2nd stitch behind the 1st one reduces the size of the 1st stitch, making it smaller, tighter, and more even.

Thus, for knitting 2 stitches together with a slant to the left, twist the 2nd stitch behind the 1st one clockwise twice, then knit 2 together through the back legs; as a result, the 1st, front, of 2, comes out reduced in size and more even. For knitting 2 stitches together with a slant to the right, twist the 1st stitch clockwise twice, instead of the 2nd one, then knit 2 together through the front legs, thus making the front stitch of 2 tighter and more even (see full description in recommendations).

Let's talk about double yarn over. This yarn over is not as frequently used as the regular one; however, it is still an essential element in openwork knitting, and therefore, knowing how to knit it well can be helpful. Any traditional method of knitting double yarn over cannot be compared with the one you are about to learn.

Usually, working double yarn over consists of knitting the 1st and purling the 2nd one, or purling the 1st and knitting the 2nd one, or purling both yarn overs through different legs, i.e., the 1st yarn over through the front leg and the 2nd one through the back leg, or the 1st yarn over through the back leg and the 2nd one through the front leg. But there is another way, which is much better than any of the described above.

Instead of knitting or purling the 1st or the 2nd yarn over, purl only the 1st yarn over and slip the 2nd one off the left needle, leaving it between the needles as is, i.e., working only 1 yarn over. In the next row, to compensate for the missing 2nd yarn over, make 1 stitch as follows: with the working yarn behind your work, insert the right needle from front to back through the hole formed by yarn overs in the previous row and pull the working yarn onto the right needle, thus returning the missing stitch (i.e., the 2nd yarn over) on the needle. This way, double yarn over comes out larger and more round than when it works other methods.

We hope you will use our tips in your work.

—Marina Molo

Recommendations

Two Ways of Knitting Stitches

Knitting through the front leg: Knit through the front leg, inserting the right needle through the stitch from left to right, purl as follows: with the working yarn in front of the stitch, insert the right needle through the stitch from back to front and wrap the working yarn counterclockwise around the tip of the right needle, then pull the working yarn with the right needle through the stitch.

Note: The purl stitch that works this way sets up the knit stitch for knitting through the front leg. This method of knitting is the most popular and known as conventional.

Knitting through the back leg: Knit through the back leg, inserting the right needle through the stitch from front to back, purl as follows: with the working yarn in front of the stitch, insert the right needle through the stitch from back to front, then move the working yarn under the right needle and pull it with the needle through the stitch. **Note:** The purl stitch that works this way sets up the knit stitch for knitting through the back leg.

Alternative Way of Knitting 2 Stitches Together for Creating More Even Stitches

Note: This method works exceptionally well for a chain of knitted 2 stockinet stitches together, which helps maintain approximately the same size of stitches in the chain from row to row, making the stitches tighter and more even.

Knitting 2 together through the front legs: turn the 1st one on the left needle clockwise twice as follows: insert the right needle through the back leg from back to front and slip the stitch onto the right needle, thus moving the back leg to the front, return this stitch onto the left needle, now the former back leg becomes the front one, then insert the right needle through the back leg 1 more time and slip the stitch onto the right needle, thus moving the back leg to the front 1 more time, leave this stitch on the right needle, insert the right needle through the back leg of the 2nd stitch from back to front and slip it onto the right needle, thus moving the back leg to the front, return both stitches onto the left needle, now knit 2 together through the front legs.

Knit 2 together through the back legs: slip the 1st stitch onto the right needle, turn the next 1 on the left needle clockwise twice as follows: insert the right needle through the back leg from back to front and slip it onto the right needle, thus moving the back leg to the front, return this stitch onto the left needle, now the former back leg becomes the front one, then insert the right needle through the back leg 1 more time and slip the stitch onto the right needle, thus moving the back leg to the front 1 more time, return this stitch onto the left needle, then return the 1st slipped stitch from the right needle to the left one, now knit 2 together through the back legs. **Note:** The same method uses for knitting 3 stitches together, with the following deference: turn the 2nd and the 3rd stitches clockwise twice and then knit 3 together as described above.

Pattern 1

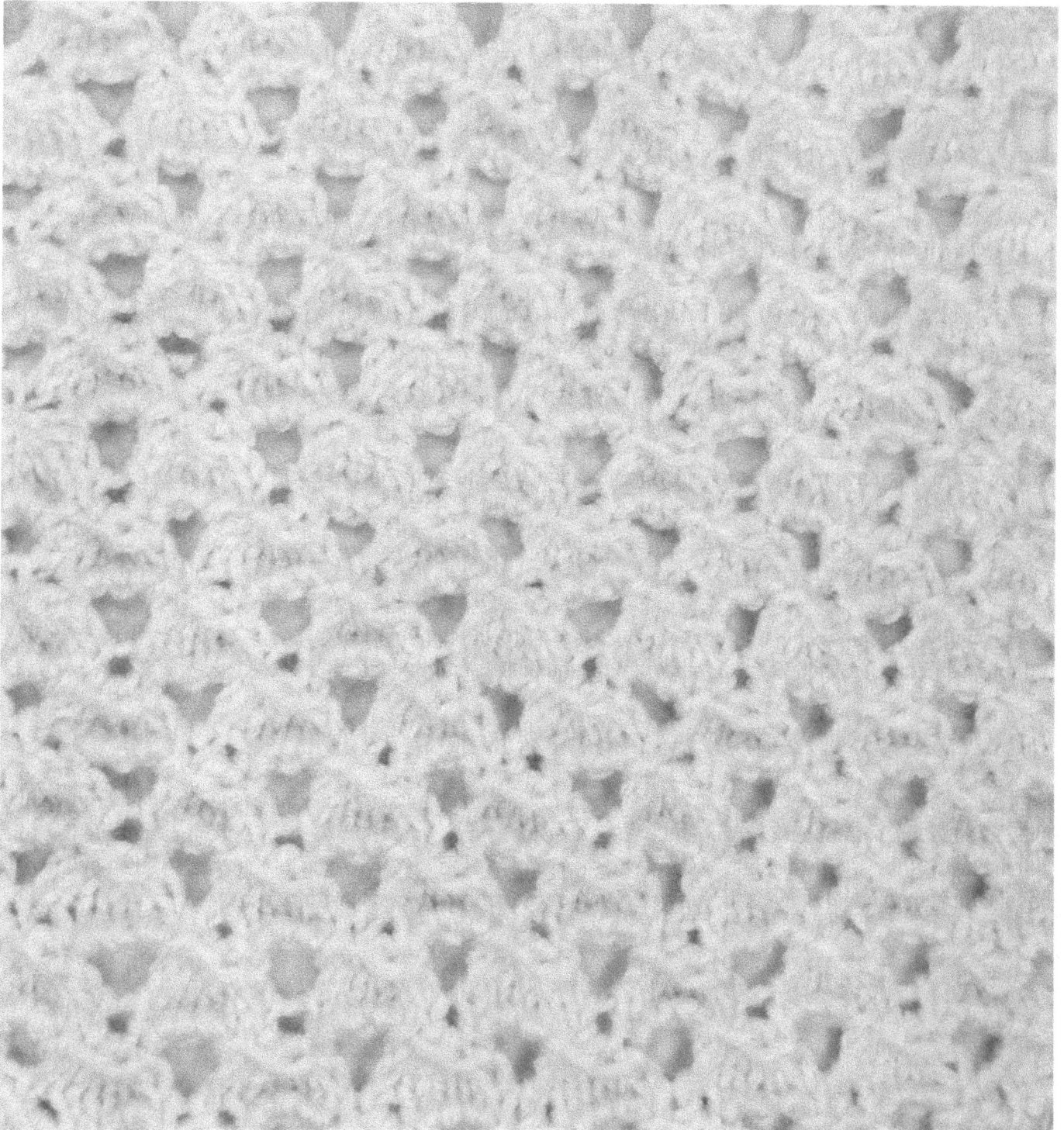

Cast on a multiple of 5, plus 2 edge stitches. Five-stitch repeat. Repeat rows: 1-8. **The edge stitches are not included in the description below and must be added. Slip the first edge stitch, purl the last one.**

Knit through the back legs, purl as follows: with the working yarn in front of the stitch, insert the right needle through the stitch from back to front, move the working yarn under the right needle and pull it with the needle through the stitch. The purl stitch that works this way sets up the knit stitch for knitting through the back leg.

Description:

Row 1: Knit all the stitches.

Row 2: *Purl 5, yarn over forward (i.e., from yourself) * repeat from * to * until the end of the row.

Row 3: *Work 4 out of yarn over made in the previous row as follows: knit 1, purl 1, knit 1, purl 1, then knit the next 5* repeat from * to * until the end of the row.

Row 4: *Knit 5 together through the **back** legs, purl 4 as follows: purl 1 through the **back** leg, purl 1 through the **front** leg, purl 1 through the **back** leg, purl 1 through the **front** leg* repeat from * to * until the end of the row.

Row 5: Knit all the stitches.

Row 6: *Yarn over forward, purl 5* repeat from * to * until the end of the row.

Row 7: *Knit 5, work 4 out of yarn over of the previous row as follows: knit 1, purl 1, knit 1, purl 1* repeat from * to * until the end of the row.

Row 8: *Purl 4 as follows: purl 1 through the **back** leg, purl 1 through the **front** leg, purl 1 through the **back** leg, purl 1 through the **front** leg, then knit 5 together through the **back** legs* repeat from * to * until the end of the row.

Repeat rows: 1-8.

Bind off as follows: Slip the edge stitch onto the right needle, knit the next 1, then insert the left needle through the slipped edge stitch, from left to right, and pass it over the knitted one, *now there is 1 stitch on the right needle, knit the next 1 (now there are 2 stitches on the right needle), insert the left needle through the 1st stitch on the right needle from left to right and pass it over the 2nd one* repeat from * to * until the end of the row.

Pattern 2

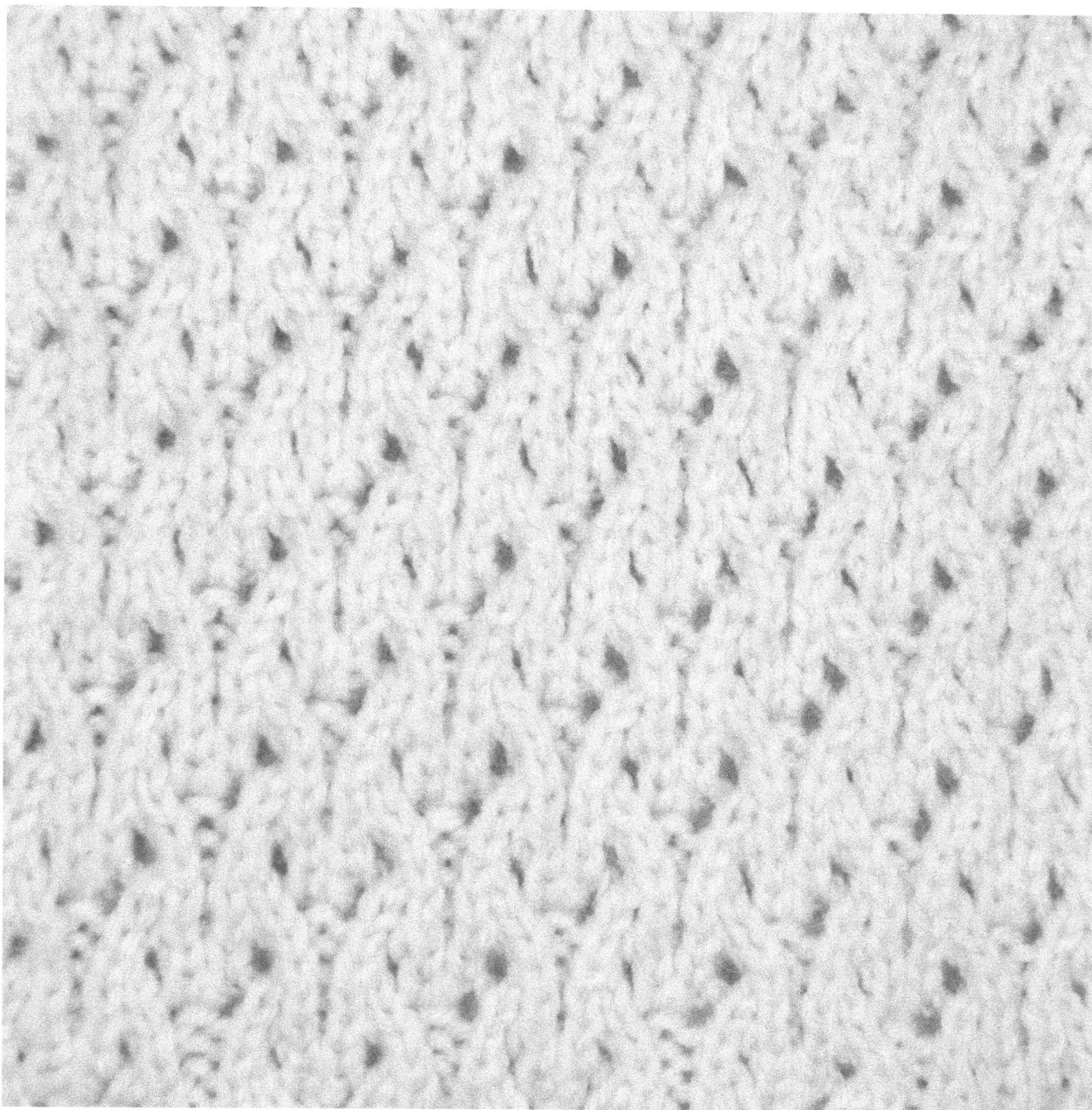

Cast on a multiple of 8, plus 1 for symmetry and 2 edge stitches. Eight-stitch repeat. Repeat rows 1-8. **The edge stitches are not included in the description below and must be added. Slip the first edge stitch, purl the last one as follows:** with the working yarn in front of the stitch, insert the right needle through the stitch from back to front, move the working yarn under the right needle and pull it with the needle through the stitch.

Knit through the front leg,purl as follows: with the working yarn in front of the stitch, insert the right needle through the stitch from back to front, wrap the working yarn forward (i.e., from yourself) around the tip of the right needle, then pull the working yarn with the right needle through the stitch. The purl stitch that works this way sets up the knit stitch for knitting through the front leg. **Needles: 2 mm.**

Description:

Row 1: *Purl 1, knit 2 together through the **back** legs as follows: insert the right needle through the first stitch from front to back and slip it onto the right needle, thus moving the front leg to the back, then return this stitch onto the left needle, now knit 2 together through the **back** legs; knit the next 1, yarn over forward (i.e., from yourself), purl 1, yarn over forward, knit 1, knit 2 together through the **front** legs* repeat from * to * until the end of the row before the edge stitch, purl 1.

Row 2: *Knit 1, purl 3 (purl yarn over of the previous row)* repeat from * to * until the end of the row before the edge stitch, knit 1.

Row 3: *Purl 1, knit 2 together through the **back** legs as described in row 1, yarn over forward, knit 1, purl 1, knit 1, yarn over forward, knit 2 together through the **front** legs* repeat from * to * until the end of the row before the edge stitch, purl 1.

Row 4: *Knit 1, purl 3 (purl yarn over of the previous row)* repeat from * to * until the end of the row before the edge stitch, knit 1.

Row 5: *Purl 1, yarn over forward, knit 1, knit 2 together through the **front** legs, purl 1, knit 2 together through the **back** legs as described in row 1, knit 1, yarn over forward* repeat from * to * until the end of the row before the edge stitch, purl 1.

Row 6: *Knit 1, purl 3 (purl the yarn over of the previous row)* repeat from * to * until the end of the row before the edge stitch, knit 1.

Row 7: *Purl 1, knit 1, yarn over forward, knit 2 together through the **front** legs, purl 1, knit 2 together through the **back** legs as described in row 1, yarn over forward, knit 1* repeat from * to * until the end of the row before the edge stitch, purl 1.

Row 8: *Knit 1, purl 3 (purl the yarn over of the previous row)* repeat from * to * until the end of the row before the edge stitch, knit 1.

Repeat rows: 1-8.

Bind off as follows: Slip the edge stitch onto the right needle, knit the next 1, then insert the left needle through the slipped edge stitch, from left to right, and pass it over the knitted stitch, *now there is 1 stitch on the right needle, knit the next 1 (now there are 2 stitches on the right needle), insert the left needle through the 1st stitch on the right needle from left to right and pass it over the 2nd one* repeat from * to * until the end of the row.

Pattern 3

Cast on a multiple of 8, plus 2, and 2 edge stitches. Eight-stitch repeat. Repeat rows: 3-14. **The edge stitches are not included in the description below and must be added. Slip the first edge stitch, knit the last one.**

Knit through the front leg; purl as follows: with the working yarn in front of the stitch, insert the right needle through the stitch from back to front, wrap the working yarn counterclockwise around the tip of the right needle, then pull it with the needle through the stitch. The purl stitch that is worked this way sets up the knit stitch to be knitted through the front leg. **Needles: 2 mm. Knit tightly.**

Description:

Row 1: Knit all the stitches.

Row 2: Purl all the stitches.

Row 3: Knit 1, *knit 2 together through the **back** legs as follows: slip the 1st stitch onto the right needle, inserting the right needle from front to back, thus moving the front leg to the back, turn the 2nd stitch forward (i.e., to yourself) as follows: insert the right needle through the back leg from back to front and slip it onto the right needle, thus moving the back leg to the front, return both stitches onto the left needle, now knit 2 together through the **back** legs, then yarn over forward (i.e., from yourself) **twice**, knit the next 2 together through the **front** legs as follows: slip the 1st stitch onto the right needle, inserting the right needle from front to back, thus moving the front leg to the back, return this stitch onto the left needle, now knit 2 together through the **front** legs, knit the next 4* repeat from * to * until the end of the row before the edge stitch, knit 1.

Row 4: Purl 1, *purl 5, work the next 2 (double yarn over of the previous row) as follows: purl the 1st one, slip the 2nd one off the left needle and leave it as is, then purl the next 1* repeat from * to * until the end of the row before the edge stitch, purl 1.

Row 5: Knit 1, *knit 2, make 1 (to return the stitch slipped off the left needle in the previous row) as follows: insert the right needle from front to back through the hole of the previous row and pull the working yarn through this hole onto the right needle, knit 5* repeat from * to * until the end of the row before the edge stitch, knit 1.

Row 6: Purl all the stitches.

Row 7: Knit all the stitches.

Row 8: Purl all the stitches.

Row 9: Knit 1, *knit 4, knit the next 2 together through the back legs, as described in row 3, then yarn over forward (i.e., from yourself) **twice**, knit the next 2 together through the **front** legs as described in row 3* repeat from * to * until the end of the row before the edge stitch, knit 1.

Row 10: Purl 1, *purl 1, work the next 2 (double yarn over of the previous row) as described in row 4, then purl the next 5* repeat from * to * until the end of the row before edge stitch, purl 1.

Row 11: Knit 1, *knit 6, make 1 (to return the stitch slipped off the left needle in the previous row) as described in row 5, then knit the next 1* repeat from * to * until the end of the row before the edge stitch, knit 1.

Row 12: Purl all the stitches.

Row 13: Knit all the stitches.

Row 14: Purl all the stitches.

Repeat rows: 3-14.

Bind off as follows: Slip the edge stitch onto the right needle, knit the next 1, then insert the left needle through the slipped edge stitch, from left to right, and pass it over the knitted stitch, *now there is 1 stitch on the right needle, knit the next 1 (now there are 2 stitches on the right needle), insert the left needle through the 1st stitch on the right needle, from left to right, and pass it over the 2nd one* repeat from * to * until the end of the row.

Pattern 4

Cast on a multiple of 14, plus 2 edge stitches. Fourteen-stitch repeat. Repeat rows: 1-12. **The edge stitches are not included in the description below and must be added. Slip the first edge stitch, purl the last one as follows:** with the working yarn in front of the stitch, insert the right needle through the stitch from back to front, move the working yarn under the right needle and pull it with the needle through the stitch.

Knit through the front leg,purl as follows: with the working yarn in front of the stitch, insert the right needle through the stitch from back to front, wrap the working yarn forward (i.e., from yourself) around the tip of the right needle, then pull the working yarn with the right needle through the stitch. The purl stitch that works this way sets up the knit stitch for knitting through the front leg. **Needles: 2.5 mm. Knit tightly.**

Description:

Row 1: *Purl 4, knit 2 together through the **front** legs, knit 2, yarn over forward (i.e., from yourself), knit 1, yarn over forward, knit 2, knit 2 together through the **back** legs as follows: slip 1 from the left needle to the right one, inserting the right needle through the stitch from front to back, thus moving the front leg of this stitch to the back, then return this stitch onto the left needle, now knit 2 together through the **back** legs, purl 1* repeat from * to * until the end of the row.

Row 2: *Knit 1, purl 9 (purl the yarn overs of the previous row), knit 4* repeat from * to * until the end of the row.

Row 3: Purl 3, knit 2 together through the **front** legs, knit 2, yarn over forward, knit 3, yarn over forward, knit 2, knit 2 together through the **back** legs as described in row 1* repeat from * to * until the end of the row.

Row 4: *Purl 11 (purl the yarn overs of the previous row), knit 3* repeat from * to * until the end of the row.

Row 5: *Purl 2, knit 2 together through the **front** legs, knit 2, yarn over forward, knit 2, knit 2 together through the **back** legs as described in row 1, knit 2, yarn over forward, knit 2* repeat from * to * until the end of the row.

Row 6: *Purl 12 (purl the yarn overs of the previous row), knit 2* repeat from * to * until the end of the row.

Row 7: *Purl 1, knit 2 together through the **front** leg, knit 2, yarn over forward, knit 1, yarn over forward, knit 2, knit 2 together through the **back** legs as described in row 1, purl 4* repeat from * to * until the end of the row.

Row 8: *Knit 4, purl 9 (purl the yarn overs of the previous row), knit 1* repeat from * to * until the end of the row.

Row 9: *Knit 2 together through the **front** legs, knit 2, yarn over forward, knit 3, yarn over forward, knit 2, knit 2 together through the **back** legs as described in row 1, purl 3* repeat from * to * until the end of the row.

Row 10: *Knit 3, purl 11 (purl the yarn overs of the previous row)* repeat from * to * until the end of the row.

Row 11: *Knit 2, yarn over forward, knit 2, knit 2 together through the **front** legs, knit 2, yarn over forward, knit 2, knit 2 together through the **back** legs as described in row 1, purl 2* repeat from * to * until the end of the row.

Row 12: *Knit 2, purl 12 (purl the yarn overs of the previous row)* repeat from * to * until the end of the row.

Bind off as follows: Slip the edge stitch onto the right needle, knit the next 1, then insert the left needle through the slipped edge stitch, from left to right, and pass it over the knitted stitch, *now there is 1 stitch on the right needle, knit the next 1 (now there are 2 stitches on the right needle), insert the left needle through the 1st stitch on the right needle from left to right and pass it over the 2nd one* repeat from * to * until the end of the row.

Pattern 5

Cast on a multiple of 8, plus 9 and 2 edge stitches. Eight-stitch repeat. Repeat rows: 1-8. **The edge stitches are not included in the description below and must be added. Slip the first edge stitch, purl the last one.**

Knit through the back leg, purl as follows: with the working yarn in front of the stitch, insert the right needle through the stitch from back to front, move the working yarn under the right needle and pull it with the needle through the stitch. The purl stitch that works this way sets up the knit stitch for knitting through the back leg. **Needles: 2.5 mm.**

Description:

Row 1: Knit 1, knit 2 together through the **front** legs as follows: turn the 1st one on the left needle clockwise twice as follows: insert the right needle through the back leg from back to front and slip it onto the right needle, thus moving the back leg to the front, return this stitch onto the left needle, now the former back leg becomes the front one, then insert the right needle through the back leg 1 more time and slip it onto the right needle, thus moving the back leg to the front 1 more time, leave this stitch on the right needle, insert the right needle through the back leg of the 2nd stitch from back to front and slip it onto the right needle, thus moving the back leg to the front, return both stitches onto the left needle, now knit 2 together through the **front** legs (**note:** this method of knitting 2 together makes the front stitch more even), yarn over forward (i.e., from yourself), knit 1, *yarn over forward (i.e., from yourself), knit 2 together through the **back** legs as follows: slip the 1st stitch onto the right needle, turn the next 1 on the left needle clockwise twice as follows: insert the right needle through the back leg from back to front and slip it onto the right needle, thus moving the back leg to the front, return this stitch onto the left needle (the former back leg becomes the front one), then insert the right needle through the back leg 1 more time and slip it onto the right needle, thus moving the back leg to the front 1 more time, return both stitches from the right needle to the left one, now knit 2 together through the **back** legs (**note:** this method of knitting 2 together makes the front stitch more even),knit 3, knit 2 together through the **front** legs as described in this row above; yarn over forward (i.e., from yourself), knit 1* repeat from * to * until the end of the row before the edge stitch—the last 5 stitches—yarn over forward (i.e., from yourself), knit 2 together through the **back** legs as described in this row above, knit 3.

Row 2: Purl all the stitches.

Row 3: Knit 2 together through the **front** legs as described in row 1, yarn over forward (i.e., from yourself), knit 2, *knit 1, yarn over forward (i.e., from yourself), knit 2 together through the **back** legs as described in row 1, knit 1, knit 2 together through the **front** legs as described in row 1, yarn over forward (i.e., from yourself), knit 2* repeat from * to * until the end of the row before the edge stitch—the last 5 stitches—knit 1, yarn over forward (i.e., from yourself), knit 2 together through the **back** legs as described in row 1, knit 2.

Row 4: Purl all the stitches.

Row 5: Knit 3, knit 2 together through the **front** legs as described in row 1, *yarn over forward (i.e., from yourself), knit 1, yarn over forward (i.e., from yourself), knit 2 together through the **back** legs as described in row 1, knit 3, knit 2 together through the **front** legs as described in row 1* repeat from * to * until the end of the row before the edge stitch—the last 4 stitches—yarn over forward (i.e., from yourself), knit 1, yarn over forward (i.e., from yourself), knit 2 together through the **back** legs as described in row 1, knit 1.

Row 6: Purl all the stitches.

Row 7: Knit 2, knit 2 together through the **front** legs as described in row 1, yarn over forward (i.e., from yourself), *knit 3, yarn over forward (i.e., from yourself), knit 2 together through the **back** legs as described in row 1, knit 1, knit 2 together through the **front** legs as described in row 1, yarn over forward (i.e., from yourself)* repeat from * to * until the end of the row before the edge stitch—the last 5 stitches—knit 3, yarn over forward (i.e., from yourself), knit 2 together through the **back** legs as described in row 1.

Row 8: Purl all the stitches.

Repeat rows: 1-8.

Bind off after the last row 8 as follows: Slip the edge stitch onto the right needle, knit the next 1, then insert the left needle through the slipped edge stitch, from left to right, and pass it over the knitted stitch, *now there is 1 stitch on the right needle, knit the next 1 (now there are 2 stitches on the right needle), insert the left needle through the 1st stitch on the right needle from left to right and pass it over the 2nd one* repeat from * to * until the end of the row.

Pattern 6

Cast on a multiple of 8, plus 2 and 2 edge stitches. Eight-stitch repeat. Repeat rows: 1-8.**The edge stitches are not included in the description below and must be added. Slip the first edge stitch, purl the last one as follows:** with the working yarn in front of the stitch, insert the right needle through the stitch from back to front, move the working yarn under the right needle and pull it with the needle through the stitch.

Knit through the front leg, purl as follows: with the working yarn in front of the stitch, insert the right needle through the stitch from back to front, wrap the working yarn forward (i.e., from yourself) around the tip of the right needle, then pull the working yarn with the right needle through the stitch. The purl stitch that works this way sets up the knit stitch for knitting through the front leg. **Needles: 2.5 mm. Knit tightly.**

Description:

Row 1: Knit 2, *knit 2, work 6 as follows: knit 1, then return this stitch onto the left needle, pass the next 5 over this returned stitch as follows: insert the right needle through 1st stitch from right to left and pass it over the returned stitch, repeat 4 more times, leave these stitches between the left and right needles as they are, then yarn over forward (i.e., from yourself), knit 1 (the same stitch that was knitted and returned onto the left needle)* repeat from * to * until the end of the row.

Row 2: *Purl 1, make 5 out of 1 (yarn over of the previous row) as follows: purl 1, yarn over forward, purl 1, yarn over forward, purl 1, then purl the next 2* repeat from * to * until the end of the row before the edge stitch, purl the last 2.

Row 3: Knit all the stitches.

Row 4: Purl all the stitches.

Row 5: *Work 6 as follows: knit 1, then return this stitch onto the left needle, pass the next 5 over this returned stitch as described in row 1, then yarn over forward (i.e., from yourself), knit 1 (the same stitch that was knitted and returned onto the left needle), then knit the next 2* repeat from * to * until the end of the row before the edge stitch, knit the last 2.

Row 6: Purl 2, *purl 3, make 5 out of 1 (yarn over of the previous row) as follows: purl 1, yarn over forward, purl 1, yarn over forward, purl 1* repeat from * to * until the end of the row.

Row 7: Knit all the stitches.

Row 8: Purl all the stitches.

Bind off as follows: After the last row 8 (Back Side), turn your work over. Front Side: Slip all the stitches from the left needle to the right one (as a result, the working yarn is at the end of the right needle); turn your work over. Back Side: Slip 2 purlwise from the left needle to the right one, insert the left needle through the 1st slipped stitch, from left to right, and pass it over the 2nd one (now there is 1 stitch on the right needle), *slip 1 purlwise from the left needle to the right one, insert the left needle through the 1st stitch on the right needle, from left to right, and pass it over the 2nd one (now there is 1 stitch on the right needle)* repeat from * to * until the end of the row.

Note: For trimming, bind off loosely, using larger needles than the working ones, as this type of binding off creates a tight chain of small edge stitches that look already finished.

Pattern 7

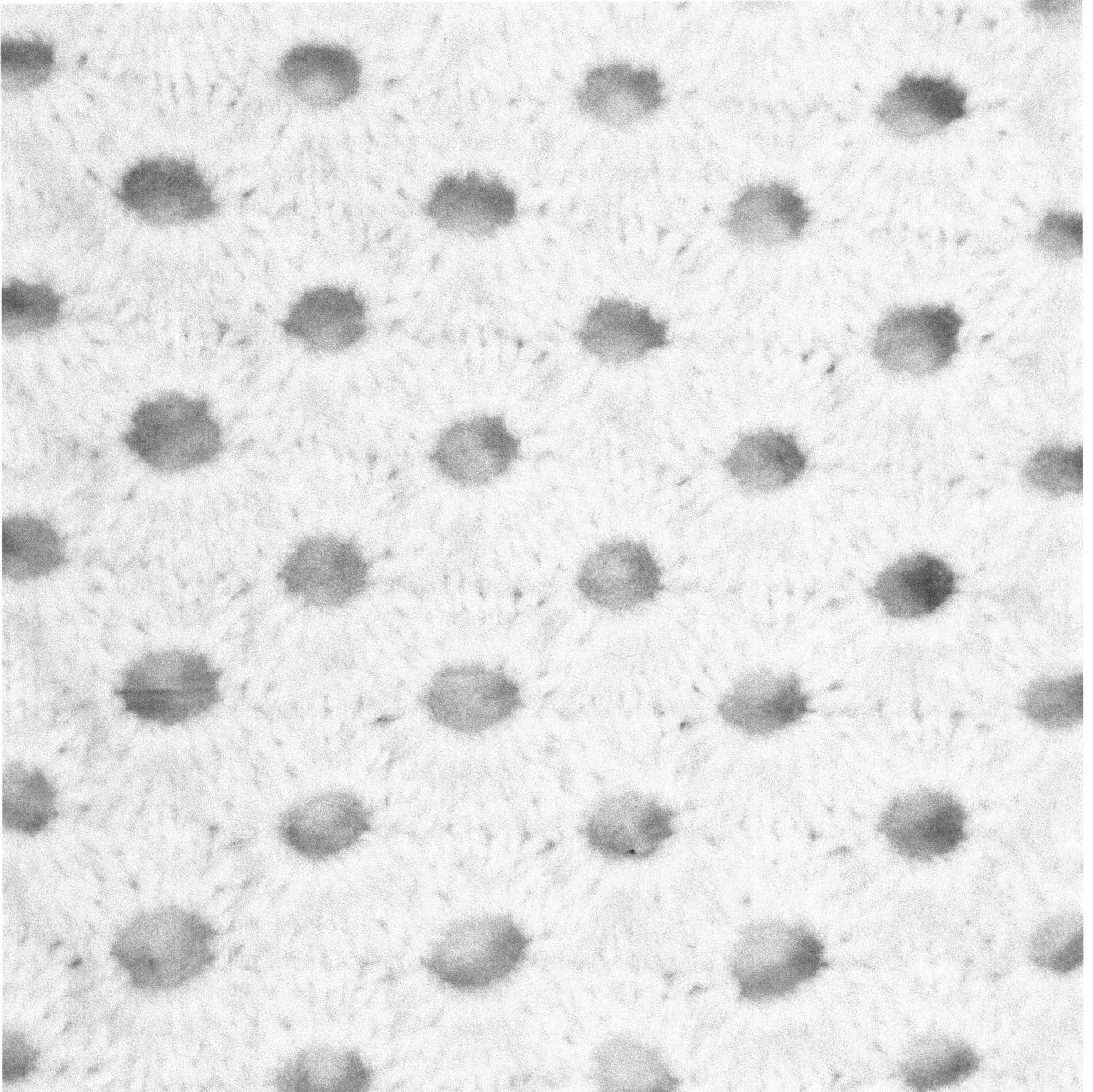

Cast on a multiple of 14, plus 3 and 2 edge stitches. Fourteen-stitch repeat. Repeat rows: 1-8. **The edge stitches are not included in the description below and must be added. Slip the first edge stitch, purl the last one as follows:** with the working yarn in front of the stitch, insert the right needle through the stitch from back to front, move the working yarn under the right needle and pull it with the needle through the stitch.

Knit through the front leg, purl as follows: with the working yarn in front of the stitch, insert the right needle through the stitch from back to front, wrap the working yarn forward (i.e., from yourself) around the tip of the right needle, then pull the working yarn with the right needle through the stitch. The purl stitch that works this way sets up the knit stitch for knitting through the front leg. **Needles: 2.5 mm. Knit tightly.**

Description:

Row 1: Knit 3, *knit 4, work 10 as follows: knit 1, then return this stitch from the right needle to the left one, pass the next 9 over this returned stitch as follows: insert the right needle through the 1st stitch from right to left and pass it over the returned stitch, repeat 8 more times, leave these stitches between the left and right needles as they are, then yarn over forward (i.e., from yourself), knit 1 (the same stitch that was knitted and returned onto the left needle)* repeat from * to * until the end of the row.

Row 2: *Purl 1, make 9 out of the next 1 (yarn over of the previous row) as follows: purl 1, yarn over forward, purl 1, yarn over forward, purl 1, yarn over forward, purl 1, yarn over forward, purl 1, then purl the next 4* repeat from * to * until the end of the row before the edge stitch, purl the last 3.

Row 3: Knit all the stitches.

Row 4: Purl all the stitches.

Row 5: *Work 10 as described in row 1, then yarn over forward (i.e., from yourself), knit 1 (the same stitch that was knitted and returned onto the left needle), then knit the next 4* repeat from * to * until the end of the row before the edge stitch, knit the last 3.

Row 6: Purl 3, *purl 5, make 9 out of the next 1 (yarn over of the previous row) as follows: purl 1, yarn over forward, purl 1, yarn over forward, purl 1, yarn over forward, purl 1, yarn over forward, purl 1* repeat from * to * until the end of the row.

Row 7: Knit all the stitches.

Row 8: Purl all the stitches.

Bind off as follows: After the last row 8 (Back Side), turn your work over. Front Side: Slip all the stitches from the left needle to the right one (as a result, the working yarn is at the end of the right needle); turn your work over. Back Side: Slip 2 purlwise from the left needle to the right one, insert the left needle through the 1st slipped stitch, from left to right, and pass it over the 2nd one (now there is 1 stitch on the right needle), *slip 1 purlwise from the left needle to the right one, insert the left needle through the 1st stitch on the right needle, from left to right, and pass it over the 2nd one (now there is 1 stitch on the right needle)* repeat from * to * until the end of the row.

Note: For trimming, bind off loosely, using larger needles than the working ones, as this type of binding off creates a tight chain of small edge stitches that look already finished.

Pattern 8

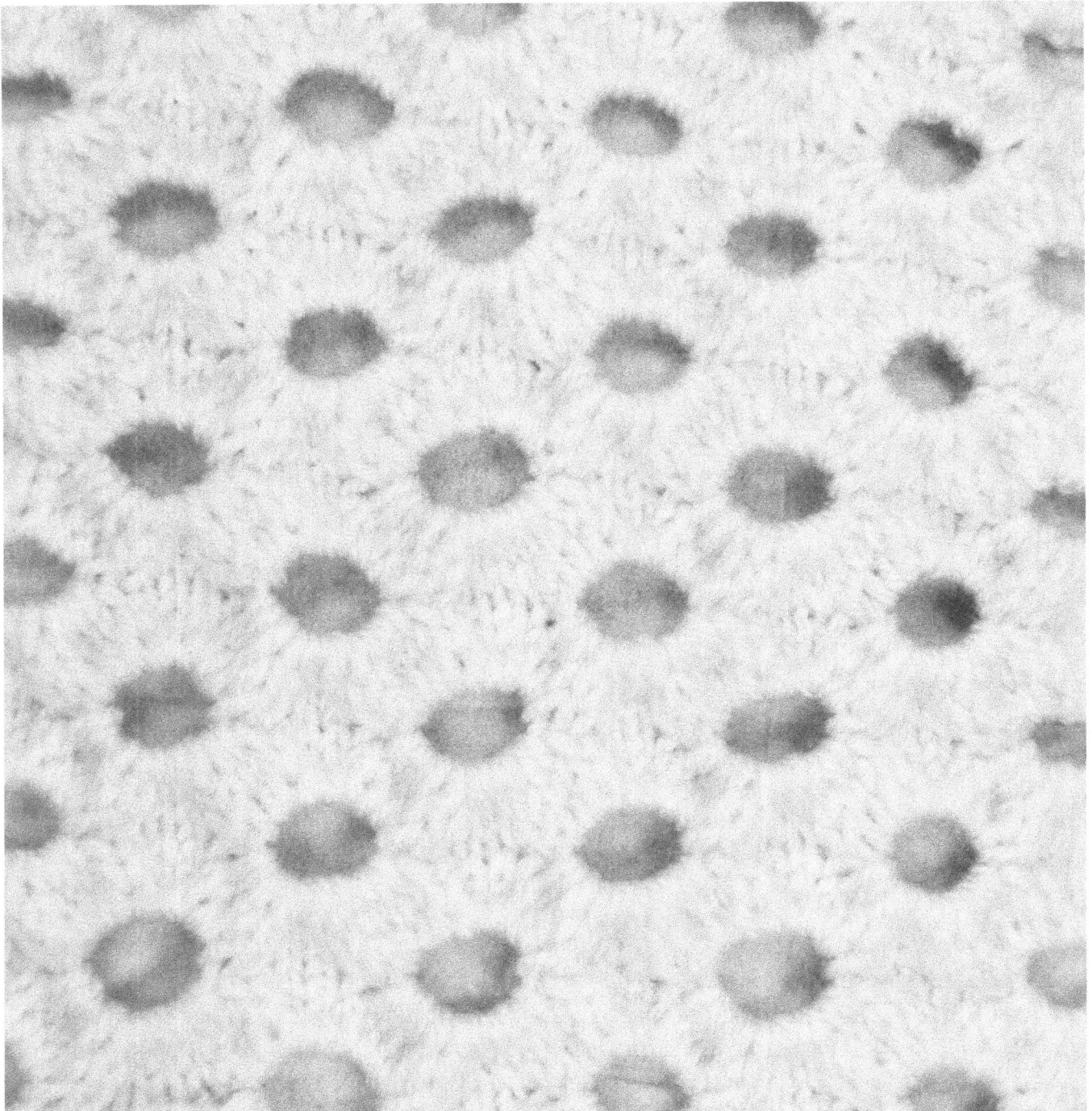

Cast on a multiple of 16, plus 3 and 2 edge stitches. Sixteen-stitch repeat. Repeat rows: 1-8. **The edge stitches are not included in the description below and must be added. Slip the first edge stitch, purl the last one as follows:** with the working yarn in front of the stitch, insert the right needle through the stitch from back to front, move the working yarn under the right needle and pull it with the needle through the stitch.

Knit through the front leg, purl as follows: with the working yarn in front of the stitch, insert the right needle through the stitch from back to front, wrap the working yarn forward (i.e., from yourself) around the tip of the right needle, then pull the working yarn with the right needle through the stitch. The purl stitch that works this way sets up the knit stitch for knitting through the front leg. **Needles: 2.5 mm. Knit tightly.**

Description:

Row 1: Knit 3, *knit 4, work 12 as follows: knit 1, then return this stitch from the right needle to the left one, pass the next 11 over this returned stitch as follows: insert the right needle through the 1st stitch from right to left and pass it over the returned stitch, repeat 11 more times, leave these stitches between the left and right needles as they are, then yarn over forward (i.e., from yourself), knit 1 (the same stitch that was knitted and returned onto the left needle)* repeat from * to * until the end of the row.

Row 2: *Purl 1, make 11 out of 1 (yarn over of the previous row) as follows: purl 1, yarn over forward, purl 1, yarn over forward, purl 1, yarn over forward, purl 1, yarn over forward, purl 1, yarn over forward, purl 1, then purl the next 4* repeat from * to * until the end of the row before the edge stitch, purl the last 3.

Row 3: Knit all the stitches.

Row 4: Purl all the stitches.

Row 5: *Work 12 as follows: knit 1, then return this stitch from the right needle to the left one, pass the next 11 over this returned stitch as described in row 1, leave them between the left and right needles as they are, then yarn over forward (i.e., from yourself), knit 1 (the same stitch that was knitted and returned onto the left needle), then knit the next 4* repeat from * to * until the end of the row before the edge stitch, knit the last 3.

Row 6: Purl 3, *purl 5, make 11 out of 1 (yarn over of the previous row) as follows: purl 1, yarn over forward, purl 1, yarn over forward, purl 1, yarn over forward, purl 1, yarn forward, purl 1, yarn over forward, purl 1* repeat from * to * until the end of the row.

Row 7: Knit all the stitches.

Row 8: Purl all the stitches.

Bind off as follows: After the last row 8 (Back Side), turn your work over. Front Side: Slip all the stitches from the left needle to the right one, now the working yarn is at the end of the right needle; turn your work over. Back Side: Slip 2 purlwise from the left needle to the right one, insert the left needle through the 1st slipped stitch, from left to right, and pass it over the 2nd one (now there is 1 stitch on the right needle), *slip 1 purlwise from the left needle to the right one, insert the left needle through the 1st stitch on the right needle, from left to right, and pass it over the 2nd one (now there is 1 stitch on the right needle)* repeat from * to * until the end of the row.

Note: For trimming, bind off loosely, using larger needles than the working ones, as this type of binding off creates a tight chain of small edge stitches that look already finished.

Pattern 9

a multiple of 23, plus 2 edge stitches. Twenty-three-stitch repeat. Repeat rows: 1-12. **The edge stitches are** ~~ded~~ **in the description below and must be added. Slip the first edge stitch, purl the last one as follows:** with ~~ng~~ yarn in front of the stitch, insert the right needle through the stitch from back to front, move the ~~rn~~ under the right needle and pull it with the needle through the stitch.

Knit through the back leg; purl as follows: with the working yarn in front of the stitch, insert the right needle through the stitch from back to front, move the working yarn under the right needle and pull it with the needle through the stitch. The purl stitch that works this way sets up the knit stitch for knitting through the back leg. **Needles: 2.5 mm.**

Description:

Row 1: *Knit 5, knit the next 2 together through the **front** legs as follows: turn the 1st stitch clockwise twice as follows: insert the right needle through the back leg from back to front and slip it onto the right needle, thus moving the back leg to the front, return it onto the left needle (now the former back leg becomes the front one), then insert the right needle through the back leg 1 more time and slip it onto the right needle, thus moving the back leg to the front 1 more time, leave it on the right needle, then insert the right needle through the back leg of the 2nd stitch from back to front and slip it onto the right needle, thus moving the back leg to the front, return both stitches onto the left needle, now knit 2 together through the **front** legs (**note:** this method of knitting 2 together makes the front stitch more even),

knit 1, yarn over forward (i.e., from yourself), knit 2 together through the **front** legs as described above, knit 1, yarn over forward, knit 1, yarn over forward, knit 1,

knit the next 2 together through the **back** legs as follows: slip the 1st stitch onto the right needle purlwise, turn the next 1 clockwise twice on the left needle as follows: insert the right needle through the back leg from back to front and slip it onto the right needle, thus moving the back leg to the front, return it onto the left needle (now the former back leg becomes the front one), then insert the right needle through the back leg 1 more time and slip it onto the right needle, thus moving the back leg to the front 1 more time, return both stitches onto the left one, now knit 2 together through the **back** legs (**note:** this method of knitting 2 together makes the front stitch more even), then yarn over forward, knit 1, knit 2 together through the **back** legs as described above, then knit 5* repeat from * to * until the end of the row.

Row 2: Purl all the stitches.

Row 3: *Knit 4, knit 2 together through the **front** legs as described in row 1, knit 1, yarn over forward, knit 2 together through the **front** legs as described in row 1, knit 1, yarn over forward, knit 3, yarn over forward, knit 1, knit 2 together through the **back** legs as described in row 1, yarn over forward, knit 1, knit 2 together through the **back** legs as described in row 1, knit 4* repeat from * to * until the end of the row.

Row 4: Purl all the stitches.

Row 5: *Knit 3, knit 2 together through the **front** legs as described in row 1, knit 1, yarn over forward, knit 2 together through the **front** legs as described in row 1, knit 1, yarn over forward, knit 5, yarn over forward, knit 1, knit 2 together through the **back** legs as described in row 1, yarn over forward, knit 1, knit 2 together through the **back** legs as described in row 1, knit 3* repeat from * to * until the end of the row.

Row 6: Purl all the stitches.

Row 7: *Knit 2, knit 2 together through the **front** legs as described in row 1, knit 1, yarn over forward, knit 2 together through the **front** legs as described in row 1, knit 1, yarn over forward, knit 7, yarn over forward, knit 1, knit 2 together through the **back** legs as described in row 1, yarn over forward, knit 1, knit 2 together through the **back** legs as described in row 1, knit 2* repeat from * to * until the end of the row.

Row 8: Purl all the stitches.

Row 9: *Knit 1, knit 2 together through the **front** legs as described in row 1, knit 1, yarn over forward, knit 2 together through the **front** legs as described in row 1, knit 1, yarn over forward, knit 9, yarn over forward, knit 1, knit 2 together through the **back** legs as described in row 1, yarn over forward, knit 1, knit 2 together through the **back** legs as described in row 1, knit 1* repeat from * to * until the end of the row.

Row 10: Purl all the stitches.

Row 11: *Knit 2 together through the **front** legs as described in row 1, knit 1, yarn over forward, knit 2 together through the **front** legs through the front legs as described in row 1, knit 1, yarn over forward, knit 11, yarn over forward, knit 1, knit 2 together through the **back** legs as described in row 1, yarn over forward, knit 1, knit 2 together through the **back** legs as described in row 1* repeat from * to * until the end of the row.

Row 12: Purl all the stitches.

Repeat rows: 1-12.

Bind off as follows: Slip the edge stitch onto the right needle, knit the next 1, then insert the left needle through the slipped edge stitch, from left to right, and pass it over the knitted stitch, *now there is 1 stitch on the right needle, knit the next 1 (now there are 2 stitches on the right needle), insert the left needle through the 1st stitch on the right needle from left to right and pass it over the 2nd one* repeat from * to * until the end of the row.

Pattern 10

Cast on a multiple of 15, plus 2 edge stitches. Fifteen-stitch repeat. Repeat rows: 1-8.**The edge stitches are not included in the description below and must be added. Slip the first edge stitch, purl the last one.**

Knit through the front leg; purl as follows: with the working yarn in front of the stitch, insert the right needle through the stitch from back to front, wrap the working yarn forward (i.e., from yourself) around the tip of the right needle, then pull the working yarn with the right needle through the stitch. The purl stitch that works this way sets up the knit stitch for knitting through the front leg. **Needles: U.S. no. 2 (2.75 mm). Use an extra-fine yarn (1 ply).**

Description:

Row 1: *Knit 3 as follows: knit 3, insert the left needle through the 1st one and pass it over the other 2 (now there are 2 stitches, instead of 3), then yarn over forward twice (i.e., from yourself)* repeat from * to * until the end of the row before the edge stitch—the last 3 stitches without the following yarn overs—knit 3, insert the left needle through the 1st one and pass it over the other 2 (now there are 2 stitches, instead of 3).

Row 2: Purl all the stitches. Work double yarn over of the previous row as follows: purl the 1st one, slip the 2nd one off the left needle and leave it as is (i.e., purl only 1 yarn over).

Row 3: Knit 1, yarn over forward twice, *knit 3 as follows: knit 3, insert the left needle through the 1st one and pass it over the other 2 (now there are 2 stitches, instead of 3), then yarn over forward twice* repeat from * to * until the end of the row before the edge stitch, knit 1.

Row 4: Purl all the stitches. Work double yarn over of the previous row as follows: purl the 1st one, slip the 2nd one off the left needle and leave it as is (i.e., purl only 1 yarn over).

Repeat rows: 1-4.

Bind off after the last row 4 as follows: Slip the edge stitch onto the right needle, knit the next 1, then insert the left needle through the slipped edge stitch, from left to right, and pass it over the knitted stitch, *now there is 1 stitch on the right needle, knit the next 1 (now there are 2 stitches on the right needle), insert the left needle through the 1st stitch on the right needle, from left to right, and pass it over the 2nd one* repeat from * to * until the end of the row.

Repeat rows: 1-8.

Bind off after the last row 8 as follows: Slip the edge stitch onto the right needle, knit the next 1, then insert the left needle through the slipped edge stitch, from left to right, and pass it over the knitted stitch, *now there is 1 stitch on the right needle, knit the next 1 (now there are 2 stitches on the right needle), insert the left needle through the 1st stitch on the right needle from left to right and pass it over the 2nd one* repeat from * to * until the end of the row.

Pattern 11

Cast on a multiple of 22, plus 2 edge stitches. Twenty-two-stitch repeat. Repeat rows: 1-12. **The edge stitches are not included in the description below and must be added. Slip the first edge stitch, purl the last one.**

Knit through the back leg; purl as follows: with the working yarn in front of the stitch, insert the right needle through the stitch from back to front, move the working yarn under the right needle and pull it with the needle through the stitch. The purl stitch that works this way sets up the knit stitch for knitting through the back leg. **Needles: 2.5 mm.**

Description:

Row 1: *Yarn over forward (i.e., from yourself), knit 5, knit the next 2 together through the **back** legs as follows: slip the 1st stitch onto the right needle purlwise, turn the next 1 clockwise twice on the left needle as follows: insert the right needle through the back leg from back to front and slip it onto the right needle, thus moving the back leg to the front, return it onto the left needle (now the former back leg becomes the front one), then insert the right needle through the back leg 1 more time and slip it onto the right needle, thus moving the back leg to the front 1 more time, return both stitches from the right needle to the left one, now knit 2 together through the **back** legs (**note:** this method of knitting 2 together makes the front stitch more even), knit 5, knit the next 2 together through the **front** legs as follows: turn the 1st stitch clockwise twice as follows: insert the right needle through the back leg from back to front and slip it onto the right needle, thus moving the back leg to the front, return it onto the left needle (now the former back leg becomes the front one), then insert the right needle through the back leg 1 more time and slip it onto the right needle, thus moving the back leg to the front 1 more time, leave it on the right needle, then insert the right needle through the back leg of the next stitch from back to front and slip it onto the right needle, thus moving the back leg to the front, return both stitches onto the left needle, now knit 2 together through the **front** legs (**note:** this method of knitting 2 together makes the front stitch more even), knit 5, yarn over forward, knit 3* repeat from * to * until the end of the row.

Row 2: Purl all the stitches.

Row 3: *Knit 1, yarn over forward, knit 5, knit 2 together through the **back** legs as described in row 1, knit 3, knit 2 together through the **front** legs as described in row 1, knit 5, yarn over forward, knit 4* repeat from * to * until the end of the row.

Row 4: Purl all the stitches.

Row 5: *Knit 2, yarn over forward, knit 5, knit 2 together through the **back** legs as described in row 1, knit 1, knit 2 together through the **front** legs as described in row 1, knit 5, yarn over forward, knit 5* repeat from * to * until the end of the row.

Row 6: Purl all the stitches.

Row 7: *Knit 3, yarn over forward, knit 5, knit 2 together through the **back** legs as described in row 1, knit 5, knit 2 together through the **front** legs as described in row 1, knit 5, yarn over forward* repeat from * to * until the end of the row.

Row 8: Purl all the stitches.

Row 9: *Knit 4, yarn over forward, knit 5, knit 2 together through the **back** legs as described in row 1, knit 3, knit 2 together through the **front** legs as described in row 1, knit 5, yarn over forward, knit 1* repeat from * to * until the end of the row.

Row 10: Purl all the stitches.

Row 11: *Knit 5, yarn over forward, knit 5, knit 2 together through the **back** legs as described in row 1, knit 1, knit 2 together through the **front** legs as described in row 1, knit 5, yarn over forward, knit 2* repeat from * to * until the end of the row.

Row 12: Purl all the stitches.

Repeat rows: 1-12.

Bind off after the last row 12 as follows: Slip the edge stitch onto the right needle, knit the next 1, then insert the left needle through the slipped edge stitch, from left to right, and pass it over the knitted stitch, *now there is 1 stitch on the right needle, knit the next 1 (now there are 2 stitches on the right needle), insert the left needle through the 1st stitch on the right needle from left to right and pass it over the 2nd one* repeat from * to * until the end of the row.

Pattern 12

Cast on a multiple of 10, plus 1 for symmetry and 2 edge stitches. Ten-stitch repeat. Repeat rows: 1-6. **The edge stitches are not included in the description below and must be added. Slip the first edge stitch tightly, purl the last one.**

Knit through the back leg; purl as follows: with the working yarn in front of the stitch, insert the right needle through the stitch from back to front, move the working yarn under the right needle and pull it with the needle through the stitch. The purl stitch that works this way sets up the knit stitch for knitting through the back leg. **Needles: 2.5 mm.**

Description:

Row 1: *Purl 1, knit 4, yarn over forward (i.e., from yourself), knit 1, yarn over forward, knit 4* repeat from * to * until the end of the row before the edge stitch, purl 1.

Row 2: *Knit 1, purl 11* repeat from * to * until the end of the row before the edge stitch, knit 1.

Row 3: *Purl 1, knit 4, yarn over forward, knit 3, yarn over forward, knit 4* repeat from * to * until the end of the row before the edge stitch, purl 1.

Row 4: *Knit 1, purl 13* repeat from * to * until the end of the row before the edge stitch, knit 1.

Row 5: *Purl 1, knit 4 together through the **front** legs, yarn over forward, knit 5, yarn over forward, knit 4 together through the **back** legs as follows: insert the right needle through each of 4 from back to front, and slip each stitch onto the right needle, thus moving back legs to the front, then return these 4 stitches onto the left needle, now knit 4 together through the **back** legs* repeat from * to * until the end of the row before the edge stitch, purl 1.

Row 6: *Knit 1, purl 9* repeat from * to * until the end of the row before the edge stitch, knit 1.

Repeat rows: 1-6.

Bind off after the last row 6 as follows: Slip the edge stitch onto the right needle, knit the next 1, then insert the left needle through the slipped edge stitch, from left to right, and pass it over the knitted stitch, *now there is 1 stitch on the right needle, knit the next 1 (now there are 2 stitches on the right needle), insert the left needle through the 1st stitch on the right needle, from left to right, and pass it over the 2nd one* repeat from * to * until the end of the row.

Pattern 13

Cast on a multiple of 3, plus 2 edge stitches. Three-stitch repeat. Repeat rows: 1-4.**The edge stitches are not included in the description below and must be added. Slip the first edge stitch, purl the last one as follows:** with the working yarn in front of the stitch, insert the right needle through the stitch from back to front, move the working yarn under the right needle and pull it with the needle through the stitch.

Knit through the front leg, purl as follows: with the working yarn in front of the stitch, insert the right needle through the stitch from back to front, wrap the working yarn forward (i.e., from yourself) around the tip of the right needle, then pull the working yarn with the right needle through the stitch. The purl stitch that works this way sets up the knit stitch for knitting through the front leg.

Description:

Row 1: Knit all the stitches.

Row 2: Purl all the stitches.

Row 3: *Yarn over forward (i.e., from yourself), knit 3 together through the **back** legs as follows: slip the first 2 onto the right needle, inserting the right needle through the front legs from left to right, slip the 3rd one onto the right needle, inserting the right needle through the front legs from left to right, then return these 3 stitches onto the left needle, now knit 3 together through the **back** legs, then yarn over forward* repeat from * to * until the end of the row.

Row 4: Purl 1, *purl 2, knit 1 through the **back** leg* repeat from * to * until the end of the row before the edge stitch, purl 2.

Repeat rows: 1-4.

Bind off after the last row 2 as follows: Slip the edge stitch onto the right needle, knit the next 1, then insert the left needle through the slipped edge stitch, from left to right, and pass it over the knitted stitch, *now there is 1 stitch on the right needle, knit the next 1 (now there are 2 stitches on the right needle), insert the left needle through the 1st stitch on the right needle, from left to right, and pass it over the 2nd one* repeat from * to * until the end of the row.

Pattern 14

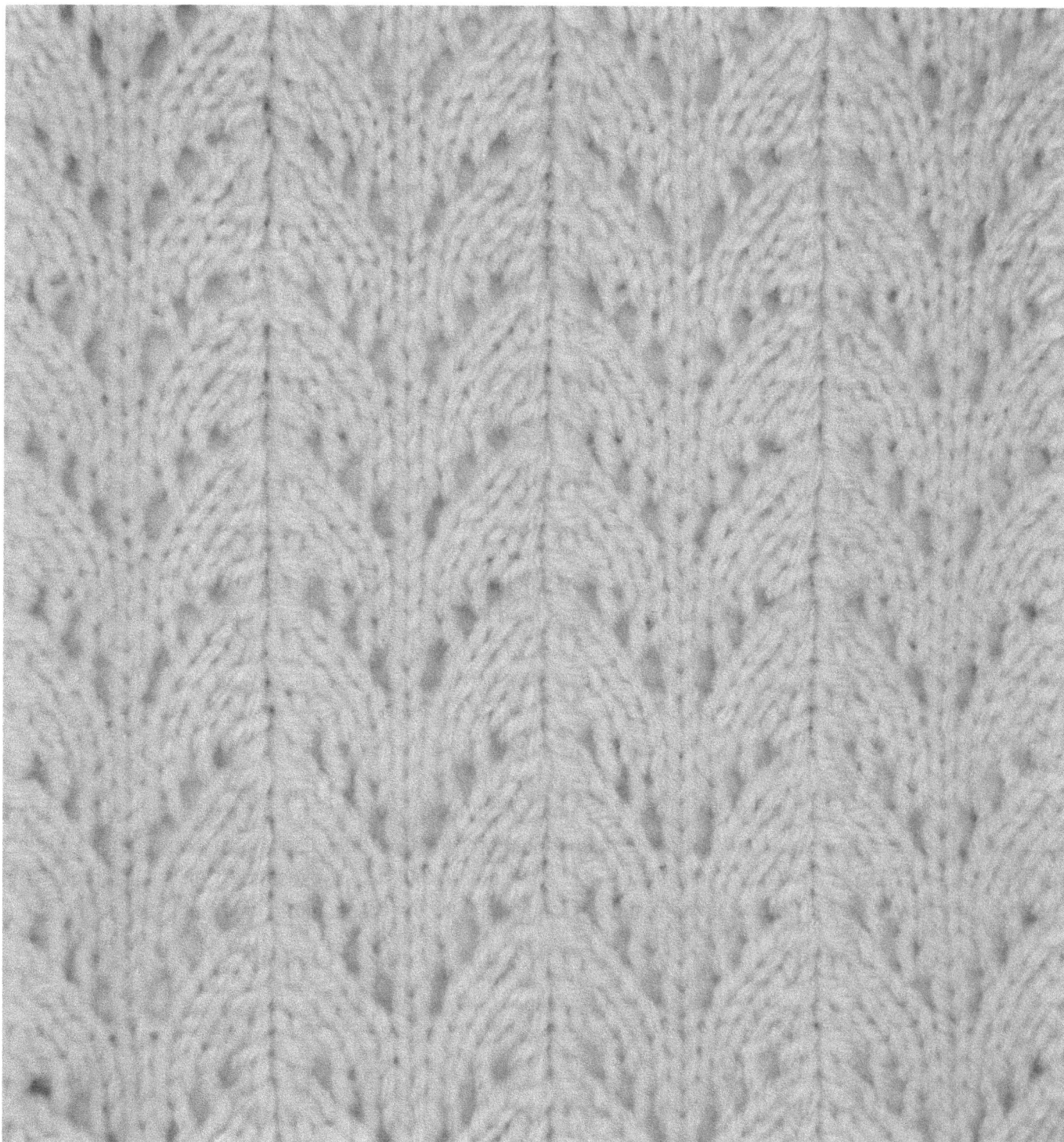

Cast on a multiple of 9, plus 2 edge stitches. Nine-stitch repeat. Repeat rows: 1-6. **The edge stitches are not included in the description below and must be added. Slip the first edge stitch, purl the last one.**

Knit through the back leg; purl as follows: with the working yarn in front of the stitch, insert the right needle through the stitch from back to front, move the working yarn under the right needle and pull it with the needle through the stitch. The purl stitch that works this way sets up the knit stitch for knitting through the back leg. **Needles: 2.5 mm.**

Description:

Row 1: *Knit 2 together through the **front** legs as follows: insert the right needle through the back leg of the 1st stitch from back to front and slip it onto the right needle, thus moving the back leg to the front, then insert the right needle through the back leg of the 2nd stitch from back to front and slip it onto the right needle, thus moving the back leg of the 2nd stitch to the front, return both stitches onto the left needle, now knit 2 together through the **front** legs, knit the next 2, yarn over forward (i.e., from yourself), knit 1, yarn over forward, knit 2, knit the next 2 together through the **back** legs* repeat from * to * until the end of the row.

Row 2: Purl all the stitches.

Row 3: *Knit 2 together through the **front** legs as described in row 1, knit 1, yarn over forward (i.e., from yourself), knit 3, yarn over forward (i.e., from yourself), knit 1, knit 2 together through the **back** legs* repeat from * to * until the end of the row.

Row 4: Purl all the stitches.

Row 5: *Knit 2 together through the **front** legs as described in row 1, yarn over forward (i.e., from yourself), knit 5, yarn over forward, knit 2 together through the **back** legs* repeat from * to * until the end of the row.

Row 6: Purl all the stitches.

Repeat rows: 1-6.

Bind off after the last row 6 as follows: Slip the edge stitch onto the right needle, knit the next 1, then insert the left needle through the slipped edge stitch, from left to right, and pass it over the knitted stitch, *now there is 1 stitch on the right needle, knit the next 1 (now there are 2 stitches on the right needle), insert the left needle through the 1st stitch on the right needle from left to right and pass it over the 2nd one* repeat from * to * until the end of the row.

Pattern 15

Cast on a multiple of 7, plus 3 and 2 edge stitches. Seven-stitch repeat. Repeat rows: 1-10.**The edge stitches are not included in the description below and must be added. Slip the first edge stitch, purl the last one as follows:** with the working yarn in front of the stitch, insert the right needle through the stitch from back to front, move the working yarn under the right needle and pull it with the needle through the stitch.

Knit through the front leg; purl as follows: with the working yarn in front of the stitch, insert the right needle through the stitch from back to front, wrap the working yarn forward (i.e., from yourself) around the tip of the right needle, then pull the working yarn with the right needle through the stitch. The purl stitch that works this way sets up the knit stitch for knitting through the front leg.

Description:

Row 1: *Knit 4, knit 2 together, knit 1, yarn over forward (i.e., from yourself) * repeat from * to * until the end of the row before the edge stitch, knit 3.

Row 2: Purl 3, *yarn over forward, purl 2, purl 2 together, purl 3* repeat from * to * until the end of the row.

Row 3: *Knit 2, knit 2 together, knit 3, yarn over forward* repeat from * to * until the end of the row before the edge stitch, knit 3.

Row 4: Purl 3, *yarn over forward, purl 4, purl 2 together, purl 1* repeat from * to * until the end of the row.

Row 5: *Knit 2 together, knit 5, yarn over forward* repeat from * to * until the end of the row before the edge stitch, knit 3.

Row 6: *Purl 4, purl 2 together as follows, to receive the knit stitch on the front side with a slant to the left: slip 2 onto the right needle, inserting the right needle through the back legs from left to right, thus moving the back legs to the front, then return both stitches onto the left needle, now purl 2 together, then purl 1, yarn over forward* repeat from * to * until the end of the row before the edge stitch, purl 3.

Row 7: Knit 3, *yarn over forward, knit 2, knit 2 together through the **back** legs as follows: slip the 1st stitch onto the right needle, inserting the right needle from front to back, thus moving the front leg to the back, then return this stitch onto the left needle, now knit 2 together through the **back** legs, then knit 3* repeat from * to * until the end of the row.

Row 8: *Purl 2, purl 2 together as described in row 6, purl 3, yarn over forward* repeat from * to * until the end of the row before the edge stitch, purl 3.

Row 9: Knit 3, *yarn over forward, knit 4, knit 2 together through the **back** legs as described in row 7, knit 1* repeat from * to * until the end of the row.

Row 10: *Purl 2 together as described in row 6, purl 5, yarn over forward* repeat from * to * until the end of the row before the edge stitch, purl 3.

Repeat rows: 1-10.

Bind off after the last row 10 as follows: Slip the edge stitch onto the right needle, knit the next 1, then insert the left needle through the slipped edge stitch, from left to right, and pass it over the knitted stitch, *now there is 1 stitch on the right needle, knit the next 1 (now there are 2 stitches on the right needle), insert the left needle through the 1st stitch on the right needle from left to right and pass it over the 2nd one* repeat from * to * until the end of the row.

Pattern 16

Cast on a multiple of 11, plus 7 and 2 edge stitches. Eleven-stitch repeat. Repeat rows: 1-18.**The edge stitches are not included in the description below and must be added. Slip the first edge stitch, purl the last one.**

Knit through the back leg; purl as follows: with the working yarn in front of the stitch, insert the right needle through the stitch from back to front, move the working yarn under the right needle and pull it with the needle through the stitch. The purl stitch that works this way sets up the knit stitch for knitting through the back leg. **Needles: 2.5 mm.**

Description:

Row 1: *Knit 8, knit the next 2 together through the **front** legs as follows: turn the 1st stitch clockwise twice as follows: insert the right needle through the back leg from back to front and slip it onto the right needle, thus moving the back leg to the front, return it onto the left needle (now the former back leg becomes the front one), then insert the right needle through the back leg 1 more time and slip it onto the right needle, thus moving the back leg to the front 1 more time, leave it on the right needle, then insert the right needle through the back leg of the 2nd stitch from back to front and slip it onto the right needle, thus moving the back leg to the front, return both stitches onto the left needle, now knit 2 together through the **front** legs (**note:** this method of knitting 2 together makes the front stitch more even), knit 1, yarn over forward (i.e., from yourself) * repeat from * to * until the end of the row before the edge stitch, knit the last 7.

Row 2: Purl 7, *yarn over forward (i.e., from yourself), purl 2, purl 2 together, purl 7* repeat from * to * until the end of the row.

Row 3: *Knit 6, knit 2 together through the **front** legs as described in row 1, knit 3 (knit the 3rd through the **front** leg), yarn over forward* repeat from * to * until the end of the row before the edge stitch, knit the last 7.

Row 4: Purl 7, *yarn over forward, purl 4, purl 2 together, purl 5* repeat from * to * until the end of the row.

Row 5: *Knit 4, knit 2 together through the **front** legs as described in row 1, knit 5 (knit the 5th through the **front** leg), yarn over forward* repeat from * to * until the end of the row before the edge stitch, knit 7.

Row 6: Purl 7, *yarn over forward, purl 6, purl 2 together, purl 3* repeat from * to * until the end of the row.

Row 7: *Knit 2, knit 2 together through the **front** legs as described in row 1, knit 7 (knit the 7th through the **front** leg), yarn over forward* repeat from * to * until the end of the row before the edge stitch, knit the last 7.

Row 8: Purl 7, *yarn over forward, purl 8, purl 2 together, purl 1* repeat from * to * until the end of the row.

Row 9: *Knit 2 together through the **front** legs as described in row 1, knit 9 (knit the 9th through the **front** leg), yarn over forward* repeat from * to * until the end of the row before the edge stitch, knit the last 7.

Row 10: *Purl 8, purl the next 2 together as follows, in order to receive the knit stitch on the front side with a slant to the left: slip the 1st one onto the right needle, insert the right needle through the 2nd one from front to back and slip it onto the right needle, thus moving the front leg to the back, return both stitches onto the left needle, insert the right needle through the back legs of both stitches from left to right, and slip them onto the right needle, thus moving the back legs to the front, return both stitches onto the left needle, now purl 2 together, then purl 1, yarn over forward* repeat from * to * until the end of the row before the edge stitch, purl the last 7.

Row 11: Knit 7, *yarn over forward, knit 2 (knit the 1st one through the **front** leg), knit the next 2 together through the **back** legs as follows: slip the 1st stitch onto the right needle, turn the 2nd one on the left needle clockwise twice as follows: insert the right needle through the stitch from back to front and slip it onto the right needle, thus moving the back leg to the front, return it onto the left needle, insert the right needle through the back leg of this stitch from back to front 1 more time and slip it onto the right needle, thus moving the back leg of this stitch to the front 1 more time, return both stitches onto the left one, now knit 2 together through the **back** legs (**note:** this method of knitting 2 together makes the front stitch more even), then knit 7* repeat from * to * until the end of the row.

Row 12: *Purl 6, purl 2 together as described in row 10, to receive the knit stitch on the front side with a slant to the left, purl 3, yarn over forward* repeat from * to * until the end of the row before the edge stitch, purl the last 7.

Row 13: Knit 7, *yarn over forward, knit 4 (knit the 1st through the **front** leg), knit 2 together through the **back** legs as described in row 11, knit 5* repeat from * to * until the end of the row.

Row 14: *Purl 4, purl 2 together as described in row 10, in order to receive the knit stitch on the front side with a slant to the left, purl 5, yarn over forward* repeat from * to * until the end of the row before the edge stitch, purl the last 7.

Row 15: Knit 7, *yarn over forward, knit 6 (knit the 1st through the **front** leg), knit 2 together through the **back** legs as described in row 11, knit 3* repeat from * to * until the end of the row.

Row 16: *Purl 2, purl 2 together as described in row 10, in order to receive the knit stitch on the front side with a slant to the left, purl 7, yarn over forward* repeat from * to * until the end of the row before the edge stitch, purl the last 7.

Row 17: Knit 7, *yarn over forward, knit 8 (knit the 1st through the **front** leg), knit 2 together through the **back** leg as described in row 11, knit 1* repeat from * to * until the end of the row.

Row 18: *Purl 2 together as described in row 10, in order to receive the knit stitch on the front side with a slant to the left, purl 9, yarn over forward* repeat from * to * until the end of the row before the edge stitch, purl the last 7.

Repeat rows: 1-18.

Bind off after the last row 18 as follows: Slip the edge stitch onto the right needle, knit the next 1, then insert the left needle through the slipped edge stitch, from left to right, and pass it over the knitted stitch, *now there is 1 stitch on the right needle, knit the next 1 (now there are 2 stitches on the right needle), insert the left needle through the 1st stitch on the right needle, from left to right, and pass it over the 2nd one* repeat from * to * until the end of the row.

Pattern 17

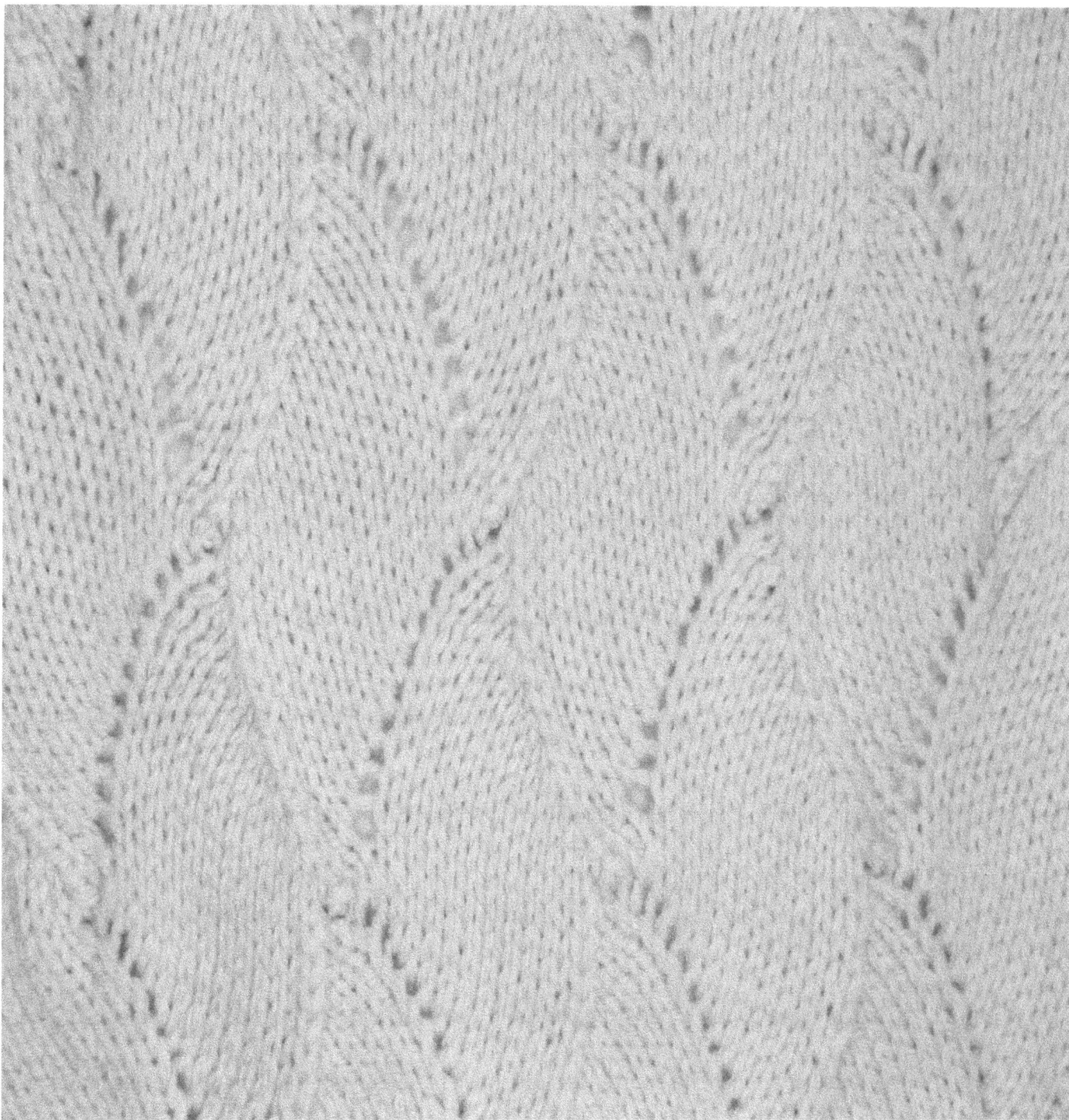

Cast on a multiple of 15, plus 11 and 2 edge stitches. Fifteen-stitch repeat. Repeat rows: 1-26. **The edge stitches are not included in the description below and must be added. Slip the first edge stitch, purl the last one.**

Knit through the back leg; purl as follows: with the working yarn in front of the stitch, insert the right needle through the stitch from back to front, move the working yarn under the right needle and pull it with the needle through the stitch. The purl stitch that works this way sets up the knit stitch for knitting through the back leg. **Needles: 2.5 mm.**

Description:

Row 1: *Knit 12, knit the next 2 together through the **front** legs as follows: turn the 1st stitch clockwise twice as follows: insert the right needle through the back leg from back to front and slip it onto the right needle, thus moving the back leg to the front, return it onto the left needle (now the former back leg becomes the front one), then insert the right needle through the back leg 1 more time and slip it onto the right needle, thus moving the back leg to the front 1 more time, leave it on the right needle, then insert the right needle through the back leg of the 2nd stitch from back to front and slip it onto the right needle, thus moving the back leg to the front, return both stitches onto the left needle, now knit 2 together through the **front** legs (**note:** this method of knitting 2 together makes the front stitch more even), knit 1, yarn over forward (i.e., from yourself)* repeat from * to * until the end of the row before the edge stitch, knit 11.

Row 2: Purl 11, *yarn over forward, purl 2, purl 2 together, purl 11* repeat from * to * until the end of the row.

Row 3: *Knit 10, knit 2 together through the **front** legs as described in row 1, knit 3 (knit the 3rd one, the former yarn over of the previous row, through the front leg), yarn over forward* repeat from * to * until the end of the row before the edge stitch, knit 11.

Row 4: Purl 11, *yarn over forward, purl 4, purl 2 together, purl 9* repeat from * to * until the end of the row.

Row 5: *Knit 8, knit 2 together through the **front** legs as described in row 1, knit 5 (knit the 5th one, the former yarn over of the previous row, through the **front** leg), yarn over forward* repeat from * to * until the end of the row before the edge stitch, knit 11.

Row 6: Purl 11, *yarn over forward, purl 6, purl 2 together, purl 7* repeat from * to * until the end of the row.

Row 7: *Knit 6, knit 2 together through the **front** legs as described in row 1, knit 7 (knit the 7th one, the former yarn over of the previous row, through the **front** leg), yarn over forward* repeat from * to * until the end of the row before the edge stitch, knit 11.

Row 8: Purl 11, *yarn over forward, purl 8, purl 2 together, purl 5* repeat from * to * until the end of the row.

Row 9: *Knit 4, knit 2 together through the **front** legs as described in row 1, knit 9 (knit the 9th one, the former yarn over of the previous row, through the **front** leg), yarn over forward* repeat from * to * until the end of the row before the edge stitch, knit 11.

Row 10: Purl 11, *yarn over forward, purl 10, purl 2 together, purl 3* repeat from *to * until the end of the row.

Row 11: *Knit 2, knit 2 together through the **front** legs as described in row 1, knit 11 (knit the 11th one, the former yarn over of the previous row, through the **front** leg), yarn over forward* repeat from * to * until the end of the row before the edge stitch, knit 11.

Row 12: Purl 11, *yarn over forward, purl 12, purl 2 together, purl 1* repeat from * to * until the end of the row.

Row 13: *Knit 2 together through the **front** legs as described in row 1, knit 13 (knit the 13th one, the former yarn over of the previous row, through the **front** leg), yarn over forward* repeat from * to * until the end of the row before the edge stitch, knit 11.

Row 14: *Purl 12, purl 2 together as follows, in order to receive the knit stitch on the front side with a slant to the left: slip the 1st one onto the right needle, insert the right needle through the 2nd one from the front to back and slip it onto the right needle, thus moving the front leg to the back, return both stitches onto the left needle, insert the right needle through the back legs of both stitches from left to right, and slip both stitches onto the right needle, thus moving the back legs to the front, return both stitches onto the left needle, now purl 2 together, then purl 1, yarn over forward* repeat from * to * until the end of the row before the edge stitch, purl 11.

Row 15: Knit 11, *yarn over forward, knit 2 (knit the 1st one through the front leg), knit the next 2 together through the **back** legs as follows: slip the 1st stitch onto the right needle, turn the 2nd one on the left needle clockwise twice as follows: insert the right needle through this stitch from back to front and slip it onto the right needle, thus moving the back leg to the front, return it onto the left needle, insert the right needle through the back leg of this stitch from back to front 1 more time and slip it onto the right needle, thus moving the back leg of this stitch to the front 1 more time, return both stitches from the right needle to the left one, now knit 2 together through the **back** legs (**note:** this method of knitting 2 together makes the front stitch more even), then knit 11* repeat from * to * until the end of the row.

Row 16: *Purl 10, purl 2 together as described in row 14, purl 3, yarn over forward* repeat from * to * until the end of the row before the edge stitch, purl 11.

Row 17: Knit 11, *yarn over forward, knit 4 (knit the 1st one through the front leg), knit 2 together through the **back** legs as described in row 15, knit 9* repeat from * to * until the end of the row.

Row 18: *Purl 8, purl 2 together as described in row 14, purl 5, yarn over forward* repeat from * to * until the end of the row before the edge stitch, purl 11.

Row 19: Knit 11, *yarn over forward, knit 6, knit 2 together as described in row 15, knit 7* repeat from * to * until the end of the row.

Row 20: *Purl 6, purl 2 together as described in row 14, purl 7, yarn over forward* repeat from * to * until the end of the row before the edge stitch, purl 11.

Row 21: Knit 11, *yarn over forward, knit 8, knit 2 together as described in row 15, knit 5* repeat from * to * until the end of the row.

Row 22: *Purl 4, purl 2 together as described in row 14, purl 9, yarn over forward* repeat from * to * until the end of the row before the edge stitch, purl 11.

Row 23: Knit 11, *yarn over forward, knit 10 (knit the 1st one through the front leg), knit 2 together as described in row 15, knit 3* repeat from * to * until the end of the row.

Row 24: *Purl 2, purl 2 together as described in row 14, purl 11, yarn over forward* repeat from * to * until the end of the row before the edge stitch, purl 11.

Row 25: Knit 11, *yarn over forward, knit 12 (knit the 1st one through the **front** leg), knit 2 together as described in row 15, knit 1* repeat from * to * until the end of the row.

Row 26: *Purl 2 together as described in row 14, purl 13, yarn over forward* repeat from * to * until the end of the row before the edge stitch, purl 11.

Repeat rows: 1-26.

Bind off after the last row 26 as follows: Slip the edge stitch onto the right needle, knit the next 1, then insert the left needle through the slipped edge stitch, from left to right, and pass it over the knitted stitch, *now there is 1 stitch on the right needle, knit the next 1 (now there are 2 stitches on the right needle), insert the left needle through the 1st stitch on the right needle from left to right and pass it over the 2nd one* repeat from * to * until the end of the row.

Pattern 18

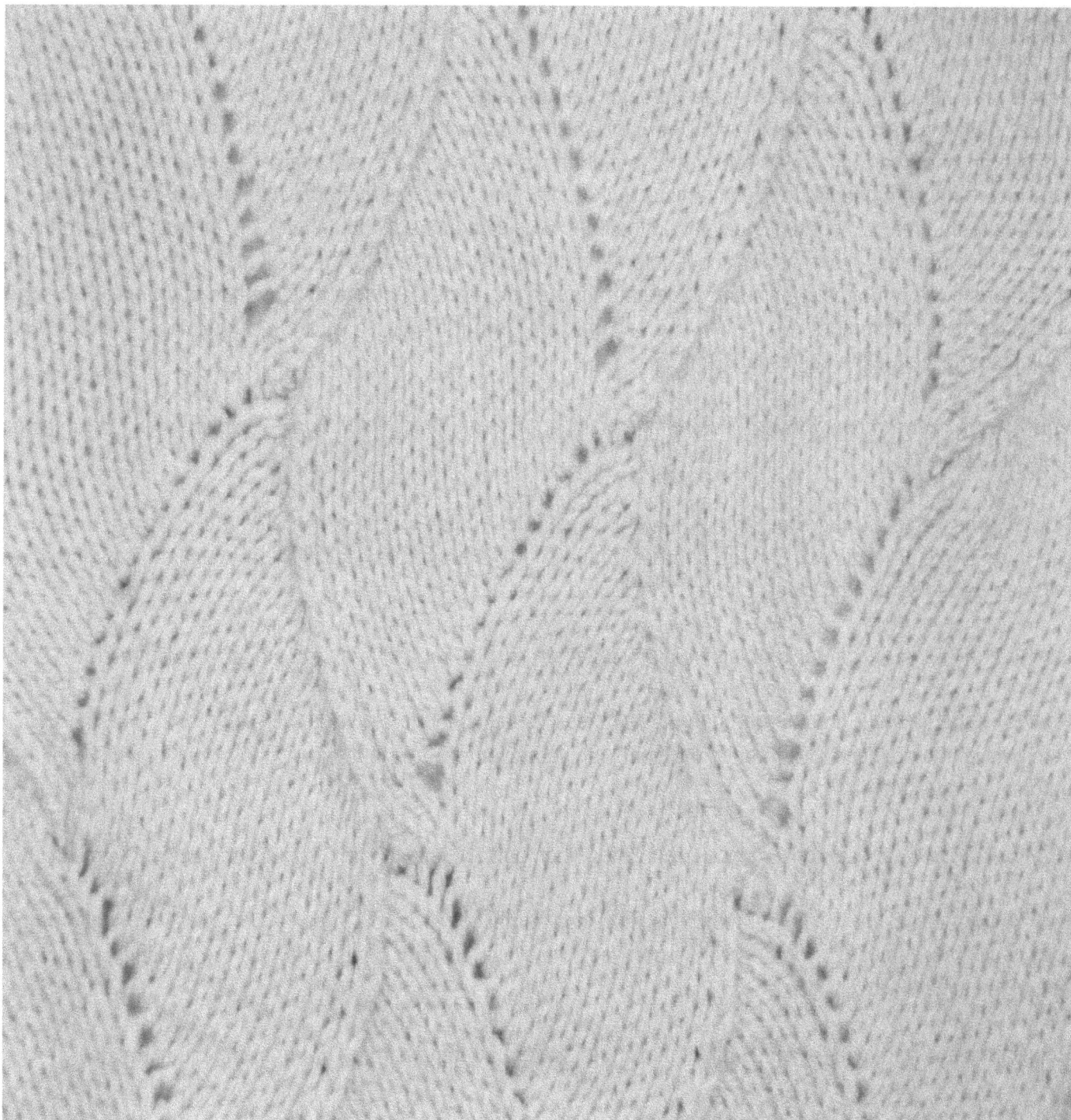

Cast on a multiple of 19, plus 15 and 2 edge stitches. Nineteen-stitch repeat. Repeat rows: 1-34.**The edge stitches are not included in the description below and must be added. Slip the first edge stitch, purl the last one.**

Knit through the back leg; purl as follows: with the working yarn in front of the stitch, insert the right needle through the stitch from back to front, move the working yarn under the right needle and pull it with the needle through the stitch. The purl stitch that works this way sets up the knit stitch for knitting through the back leg. **Needles: 2.5 mm.**

Description:

Row 1: *Knit 16, knit the next 2 together through the **front** legs as follows: turn the 1st stitch clockwise twice as follows: insert the right needle through the back leg from back to front and slip it onto the right needle, thus moving the back leg to the front, return it onto the left needle (now the former back leg becomes the front one), then insert the right needle through the back leg 1 more time and slip it onto the right needle, thus moving the back leg to the front 1 more time, leave it on the right needle, then insert the right needle through the back leg of the 2nd stitch from back to front and slip it onto the right needle, thus moving the back leg to the front, return both stitches onto the left needle, now knit 2 together through the **front** legs (**note:** this method of knitting 2 together makes the front stitch more even), then knit 1, yarn over forward (i.e., from yourself)* repeat from * to * until the end of the row before the edge stitch, knit 15.

Row 2: Purl 15, *yarn over forward (i.e., from yourself), purl 2, purl 2 together, purl 15* repeat from * to * until the end of the row.

Row 3: *Knit 14, knit 2 together through the **front** legs as described in row 1, knit 3 (knit the 3rd one, the former yarn over of the previous row, through the **front** leg), yarn over forward* repeat from * to * until the end of the row before the edge stitch, knit 15.

Row 4: Purl 15, *yarn over forward, purl 4, purl 2 together, purl 13* repeat from * to * until the end of the row.

Row 5: *Knit 12, knit 2 together through the **front** legs as described in row 1, knit 5 (knit the 5th one, the former yarn over of the previous row, through the **front** leg), yarn over forward* repeat from * to * until the end of the row before the edge stitch, knit 15.

Row 6: Purl 15, *yarn over forward, purl 6, purl 2 together, purl 11* repeat from * to * until the end of the row.

Row 7: *Knit 10, knit 2 together through the **front** legs as described in row 1, knit 7 (knit the 7th one, the former yarn over of the previous row, through the **front** leg), yarn over forward* repeat from * to * until the end of the row before the edge stitch, knit 15.

Row 8: Purl 15, *yarn over forward, purl 8, purl 2 together, purl 9* repeat from * to * until the end of the row.

Row 9: *Knit 8, knit 2 together through the **front** legs as described in row 1, knit 9 (knit the 9th one, the former yarn over of the previous row, through the **front** leg), yarn over forward* repeat from * to * until the end of the row before the edge stitch, knit 15.

Row 10: Purl 15, *yarn over forward, purl 10, purl 2 together, purl 7* repeat from *to * until the end of the row.

Row 11: *Knit 6, knit 2 together through the **front** legs as described in row 1, knit 11 (knit the 11th one, the former yarn over of the previous row, through the front leg), yarn over forward* repeat from * to * until the end of the row before the edge stitch, knit 15.

Row 12: Purl 15, *yarn over forward, purl 12, purl 2 together, purl 5* repeat from * to * until the end of the row.

Row 13: *Knit 4, knit 2 together through the **front** legs as described in row 1, knit 13 (knit the 13th one, the former yarn over of the previous row, through the **front** leg), yarn over forward* repeat from * to * until the end of the row before the edge stitch, knit 15.

Row 14: Purl 15, *yarn over forward, purl 14, purl 2 together, purl 3* repeat from * to * until the end of the row.

Row 15: *Knit 2, knit 2 together through the **front** legs as described in row 1, knit 15 (knit the 15th one, the former yarn over of the previous row, through the **front** leg), yarn over forward* repeat from * to * until the end of the row before the edge stitch knit 15.

Row 16: Purl 15, *yarn over forward, purl 16, purl 2 together, purl 1* repeat from * to * until the end of the row.

Row 17: *Knit 2 together through the **front** legs as described in row 1, knit 17, yarn over forward* repeat from * to * until the end of the row before the edge stitch, knit 15.

Row 18: *Purl 16, purl 2 together as follows, to receive the knit stitch on the front side with a slant to the left: slip the 1st one onto the right needle, insert the right needle through the 2nd stitch from the front to back and slip it onto the right needle, thus moving the front leg to the back, return both stitches onto the left needle, insert the right needle through the back legs of both stitches from left to right and slip them onto the right needle, thus moving the back legs to the front, return both stitches onto the left needle, now purl 2 together, then purl 1, yarn over forward* repeat from * to * until the end of the row before the edge stitch, purl 15.

Row 19: Knit 15, *yarn over forward, knit 2 (knit the 1st one, the former yarn over of the previous row, through the front leg), knit the next 2 together through the **back** legs as follows, to receive the front stitch more even: slip the 1st stitch onto the right needle, turn the 2nd one on the left needle clockwise twice as follows: insert the right needle through this stitch from back to front and slip it onto the right needle, thus moving the back leg to the front, return it onto the left needle, insert the right needle through the back leg of this stitch from back to front 1 more time and slip it onto the right needle, thus moving the back leg of this stitch to the front 1 more time, return both stitches from the right needle to the left one, now knit 2 together through the **back** legs, then knit 15* repeat from * to * until the end of the row.

Row 20: *Purl 14, purl 2 together as described in row 18, purl 3, yarn over forward* repeat from * to * until the end of the row before the edge stitch, purl 15.

Row 21: Knit 15, *yarn over forward, knit 4 (knit the 1st one, the former yarn over of the previous row, through the **front** leg), knit the next 2 together through the **back** legs as described in row 19, knit 13* repeat from * to * until the end of the row.

Row 22: *Purl 12, purl 2 together as described in row 18, purl 5, yarn over forward* repeat from * to * until the end of the row before the edge stitch, purl 15.

Row 23: Knit 15, *yarn over forward, knit 6 (knit the 1st one, the former yarn over of the previous row, through the **front** leg), knit 2 together through the **back** legs as described in row 19, knit 11* repeat from * to * until the end of the row.

Row 24: *Purl 10, purl 2 together as described in row 18, purl 7, yarn over forward* repeat from * to * until the end of the row before the edge stitch, purl 15.

Row 25: Knit 15, *yarn over forward, knit 8 (knit the 1st one, the former yarn over of the previous row, through the **front** leg), knit 2 together through the **back** legs as described in row 19, knit 9* repeat from * to * until the end of the row.

Row 26: *Purl 8, purl 2 together as described in row 18, purl 9, yarn over forward* repeat from * to * until the end of the row before the edge stitch, purl 15.

Row 27: Knit 15, *yarn over forward, knit 10 (knit the 1st one, the former yarn over of the previous row, through the **front** leg), knit 2 together through the **back** legs as described in row 19, knit 7* repeat from * to * until the end of the   row.

Row 28: *Purl 6, purl 2 together as described in row 18, purl 11, yarn over forward * repeat from * to * until the end of the row before the edge stitch, purl 15.

Row 29: Knit 15, *yarn over forward, knit 12 (knit the 1st one, the former yarn over of the previous row, through the front leg), knit 2 together through the **back** legs as described in row 19, knit 5* repeat from * to * until the end of the row.

Row 30: *Purl 4, purl 2 together as described in row 18, purl 13, yarn over forward* repeat from * to * until the end of the row before the edge stitch, purl 15.

Row 31: Knit 15, *yarn over forward, knit 14 (knit the 1st one, the former yarn over of the previous row, through the **front** leg), knit 2 together as described in row 19, knit 3* repeat from * to * until the end of the row.

Row 32: *Purl 2, purl 2 together as described in row 18, purl 15, yarn over forward* repeat from * to * until the end of the row before the edge stitch, purl 15.

Row 33: Knit 15, *yarn over forward, knit 16 (knit the 1st one, the former yarn over of the previous row, through the **front** leg), knit 2 together through the **back** legs as described in row 19, knit 1* repeat from * to * until the end of the row.

Row 34: *Purl 2 together as described in row 18, purl 17, yarn over forward* repeat from * to * until the end of the row before the edge stitch, purl 15.

Repeat rows: 1-34.

Bind off after the last row 34 as follows: Slip the edge stitch onto the right needle, knit the next 1, then insert the left needle through the slipped edge stitch, from left to right, and pass it over the knitted stitch, *now there is 1 stitch on the right needle, knit the next 1 (now there are 2 stitches on the right needle), insert the left needle through the 1st stitch on the right needle, from left to right, and pass it over the 2nd one* repeat from * to * until the end of the row.

Pattern 19

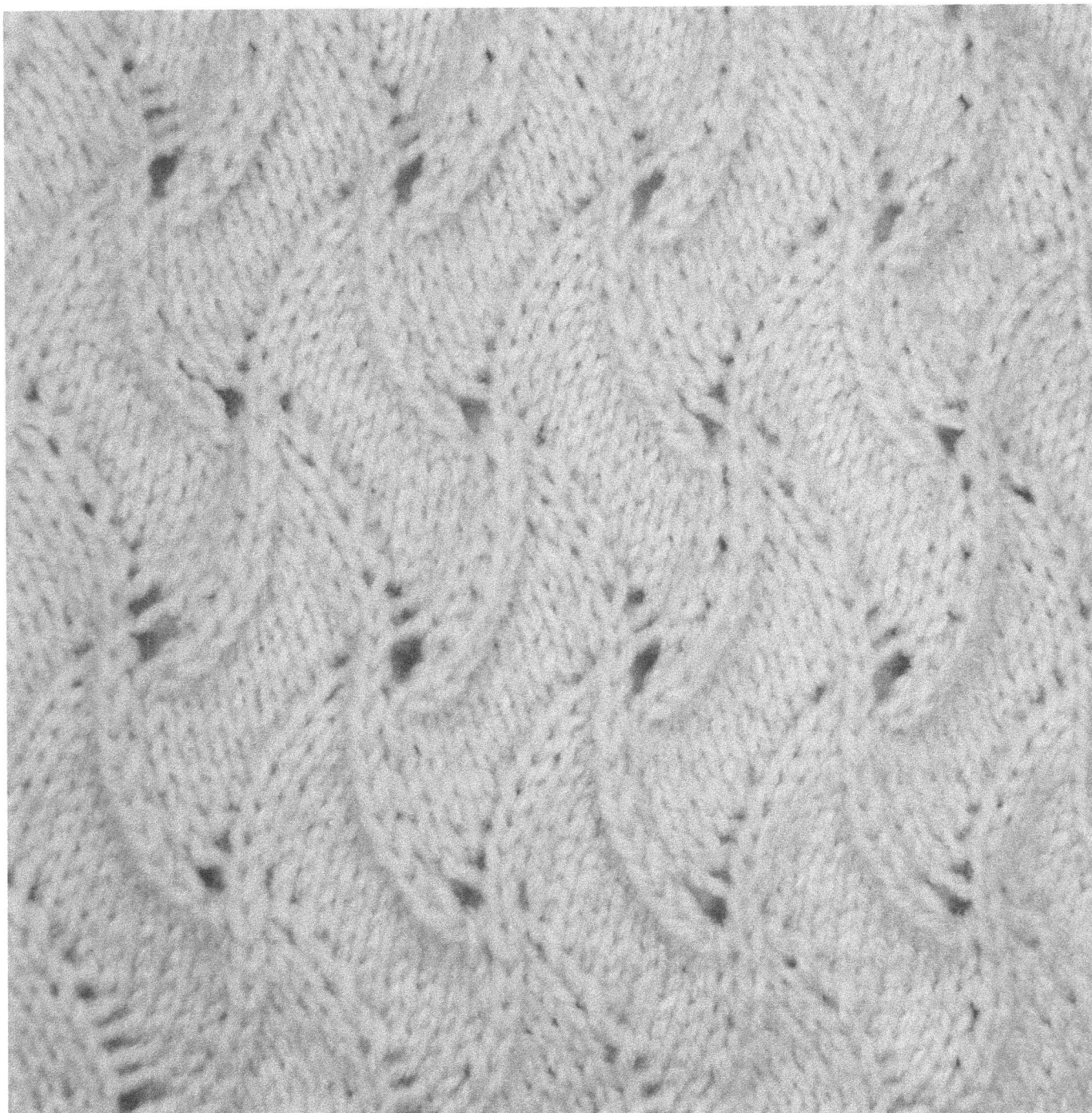

Cast on a multiple of 10, plus 2 edge stitches. Ten-stitch repeat. Repeat rows: 1-18.**The edge stitches are not included in the description below and must be added. Slip the first edge stitch, purl the last one as follows:** with the working yarn in front of the stitch, insert the right needle through the stitch from back to front, move the working yarn under the right needle and pull it with the needle through the stitch.

Knit through the front leg; purl as follows: with the working yarn in front of the stitch, insert the right needle through the stitch from back to front, wrap the working yarn forward (i.e., from yourself) around the tip of the right needle, then pull the working yarn with the right needle through the stitch. The purl stitch that works this way sets up the knit stitch for knitting through the front leg.

Description:

Row 1: *Yarn over forward (i.e., from yourself), knit 8, knit 2 together* repeat from * to * until the end of the row.

Row 2: *Purl 2 together, purl 7, yarn over forward, purl 1* repeat from * to * until the end of the row.

Row 3: *Knit 2, yarn over forward, knit 6, knit 2 together* repeat from * to * until the end of the row.

Row 4: *Purl 2 together, purl 5, yarn over forward, purl 3* repeat from * to * until the end of the row.

Row 5: *Knit 4, yarn over forward, knit 4, knit 2 together* repeat from * to * until the end of the row.

Row 6: *Purl 2 together, purl 3, yarn over forward, purl 5* repeat from * to * until the end of the row.

Row 7: *Knit 6, yarn over forward, knit 2, knit 2 together* repeat from * to * until the end of the row.

Row 8: *Purl 2 together, purl 1, yarn over forward, purl 7* repeat from * to * until the end of the row.

Row 9: *Knit 8, yarn over forward, knit 2 together* repeat from * to * until the end of the row.

Row 10: *Yarn over forward, purl 8, purl 2 together as follows, to receive the knit stitch on the front side with a slant to the left: slip 2 onto the right needle, inserting the right needle through the back legs from left to right, thus moving the back legs to the front, then return both stitches onto the left needle, now purl 2 together* repeat from * to * until the end of the row.

Row 11: *Knit 2 together through the **back** legs as follows: slip the 1st stitch onto the right needle, inserting the right needle from front to back, thus moving the front leg to the back, then return this stitch onto the left needle, now knit 2 together through the **back** legs, knit 7, yarn over forward, knit 1* repeat from * to * until the end of the row.

Row 12: *Purl 2, yarn over forward, purl 6, purl 2 together as described in row 10* repeat from * to * until the end of the row.

Row 13: *Knit 2 together through the **back** legs as described in row 11, knit 5, yarn over forward, knit 3* repeat from * to * until the end of the row.

Row 14: *Purl 4, yarn over forward, purl 4, purl 2 together as described in row 10* repeat from * to * until the end of the row.

Row 15: *Knit 2 together through the **back** legs as described in row 11, knit 3, yarn over forward, knit 5* repeat from * to * until the end of the row.

Row 16: *Purl 6, yarn over forward, purl 2, purl 2 together as described in row 10* repeat from * to * until the end of the row.

Row 17: *Knit 2 together through the **back** legs as described in row 11, knit 1, yarn over forward, knit 7* repeat from * to * until the end of the row.

Row 18: *Purl 8, yarn over forward, purl 2 together as described in row 10* repeat from * to * until the end of the row.

Repeat rows: 1-18.

Bind off after the last row 18 as follows: Slip the edge stitch onto the right needle, knit the next 1, then insert the left needle through the slipped edge stitch, from left to right, and pass it over the knitted stitch, *now there is 1 stitch on the right needle, knit the next 1 (now there are 2 stitches on the right needle), insert the left needle through the 1st stitch on the right needle from left to right and pass it over the 2nd one* repeat from * to * until the end of the row.

Pattern 20

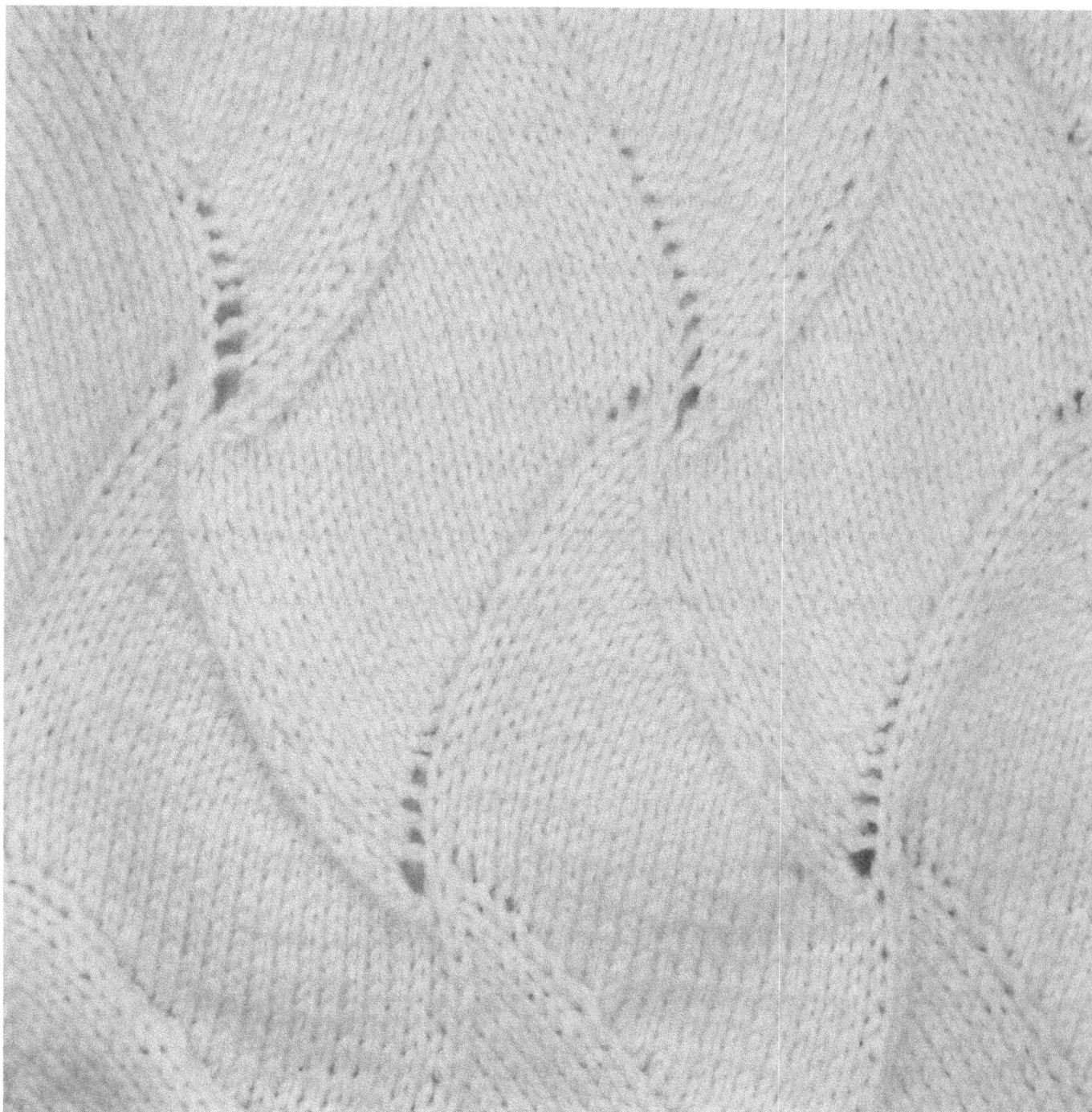

Cast on a multiple of 22, plus 2 edge stitches. Twenty-two-stitch repeat. Repeat rows: 1-42.**The edge stitches are not included in the description below and must be added. Slip the first edge stitch, purl the last one as follows:** with the working yarn in front of the stitch, insert the right needle through the stitch from back to front, move the working yarn under the right needle and pull it with the needle through the stitch.

Knit through the front leg; purl as follows: with the working yarn in front of the stitch, insert the right needle through the stitch from back to front, wrap the working yarn forward (i.e., from yourself) around the tip of the right needle, then pull the working yarn with the right needle through the stitch. The purl stitch that works this way sets up the knit stitch for knitting through the front leg. **Needles: 2.5 mm. Knit tightly.**

Description:

Row 1: *Yarn over forward (i.e., from yourself), knit 20, knit 2 together* repeat from * to * until the end of the row.

Row 2: *Purl 2 together, purl 19, yarn over forward, purl 1* repeat from * to * until the end of the row.

Row 3: *Knit 2, yarn over forward, knit 18, knit 2 together* repeat from * to * until the end of the row.

Row 4: *Purl 2 together, purl 17, yarn over forward, purl 3* repeat from * to * until the end of the row.

Row 5: *Knit 4, yarn over forward, knit 16, knit 2 together* repeat from * to * until the end of the row.

Row 6: *Purl 2 together, purl 15, yarn over forward, purl 5* repeat from * to * until the end of the row.

Row 7: *Knit 6, yarn over forward, knit 14, knit 2 together* repeat from * to * until the end of the row.

Row 8: *Purl 2 together, purl 13, yarn over forward, purl 7* repeat from * to * until the end of the row.

Row 9: *Knit 8, yarn over forward, knit 12, knit 2 together* repeat from * to * until the end of the row.

Row 10: *Purl 2 together, purl 11, yarn over forward, purl 9* repeat from * to * until the end of the row.

Row 11: *Knit 10, yarn over forward, knit 10, knit 2 together* repeat from * to * until the end of the row.

Row 12: *Purl 2 together, purl 9, yarn over forward, purl 11* repeat from * to * until the end of the row.

Row 13: *Knit 12, yarn over forward, knit 8, knit 2 together* repeat from * to * until the end of the row.

Row 14: *Purl 2 together, purl 7, yarn over forward, purl 13* repeat from * to * until the end of the row.

Row 15: *Knit 14, yarn over forward, knit 6, knit 2 together* repeat from * to * until the end of the row.

Row 16: *Purl 2 together, purl 5, yarn over forward, purl 15* repeat from * to * until the end of the row.

Row 17: *Knit 16, yarn over forward, knit 4, knit 2 together* repeat from * to * until the end of the row.

Row 18: *Purl 2 together, purl 3, yarn over forward, purl 17* repeat from * to * until the end of the row.

Row 19: *Knit 18, yarn over forward, knit 2, knit 2 together* repeat from * to * until the end of the row.

Row 20: *Purl 2 together, purl 1, yarn over forward, purl 19* repeat from * to * until the end of the row.

Row 21: *Knit 20, yarn over forward, knit 2 together* repeat from * to * until the end of the row.

Row 22: *Yarn over forward, purl 20, purl 2 together as follows, to receive the knit stitch on the front side with a slant to the left: slip 2 onto the right needle, inserting the right needle through the back legs from left to right, thus moving the back legs to the front, return both stitches onto the left needle, now purl 2 together* repeat from * to * until the end of the row.

Row 23: *Knit 2 together through the **back** legs as follows: slip the 1st stitch onto the right needle, inserting the right needle from front to back, thus moving the front leg to the back, return this stitch onto the left needle, now knit 2 together through the back legs, knit 19, yarn over forward, knit 1* repeat from * to * until the end of the row.

Row 24: *Purl 2, yarn over forward, purl 18, purl 2 together as described in row 22* repeat from * to * until the end of the row.

Row 25: *Knit 2 together through the **back** legs as described in row 23, knit 17, yarn over forward, knit 3* repeat from * to * until the end of the row.

Row 26: *Purl 4, yarn over forward, purl 16, purl 2 together as described in row 22* repeat from * to * until the end of the row.

Row 27: *Knit 2 together through the **back** legs as described in row 23, knit 15, yarn over forward, knit 5* repeat from * to * until the end of the row.

Row 28: *Purl 6, yarn over forward, purl 14, purl 2 together as described in row 22* repeat from * to * until the end of the row.

Row 29: *Knit 2 together through the **back** legs as described in row 23, knit 13, yarn over forward, knit 7* repeat from * to * until the end of the row.

Row 30: *Purl 8, yarn over forward, purl 12, purl 2 together as described in row 22* repeat from * to * until the end of the row.

Row 31: *Knit 2 together through the **back** legs as described in row 23, knit 11, yarn over forward, knit 9* repeat from * to * until the end of the row.

Row 32: *Purl 10, yarn over forward, purl 10, purl 2 together as described in row 22* repeat from * to * until the end of the row.

Row 33: *Knit 2 together through the **back** legs as described in row 23, knit 9, yarn over forward, knit 11* repeat from * to * until the end of the row.

Row 34: *Purl 12, yarn over forward, purl 8, purl 2 together as described in row 22* repeat from * to * until the end of the row.

Row 35: *Knit 2 together through the **back** legs as described in row 23, knit 7, yarn over forward, knit 13* repeat from * to * until the end of the row.

Row 36: *Purl 14, yarn over forward, purl 6, purl 2 together as described in row 22* repeat from * to * until the end of the row.

Row 37: *Knit 2 together through the **back** legs as described in row 23, knit 5, yarn over forward, knit 15* repeat from * to * until the end of the row.

Row 38: *Purl 16, yarn over forward, purl 4, purl 2 together as described in row 22* repeat from * to * until the end of the row.

Row 39: *Knit 2 together through the **back** legs as described in row 23, knit 3, yarn over forward, knit 17* repeat from * to * until the end of the row.

Row 40: *Purl 18, yarn over forward, purl 2, purl 2 together as described in row 22* repeat from * to * until the end of the row.

Row 41: *Knit 2 together through the **back** legs as described in row 23, knit 1, yarn over forward, knit 19* repeat from * to * until the end of the row.

Row 42: *Purl 20, yarn over forward, purl 2 together as described in row 22* repeat from * to * until the end of the row.

Repeat rows: 1-42.

ᴉd off after the last row 42 as follows: Slip the edge stitch onto the right needle, knit the next 1, then insert the needle through the slipped edge stitch, from left to right, and pass it over the knitted stitch, *now there is 1 h on the right needle, knit the next 1 (now there are 2 stitches on the right needle), insert the left needle ᵍh the 1st stitch on the right needle from left to right and pass it over the 2nd one* repeat from * to * until the f the row.

Pattern 21

Cast on a multiple of 15, plus 8 and 2 edge stitches. Fifteen-stitch repeat. Repeat rows: 1-12. **The edge stitches are not included in the description below and must be added. Slip the first edge stitch, purl the last one.**

Knit through the back leg; purl as follows: with the working yarn in front of the stitch, insert the right needle through the stitch from back to front, move the working yarn under the right needle and pull it with the needle through the stitch. The purl stitch that works this way sets up the knit stitch for knitting through the back leg. **Needles: 2.5 mm.**

Description:

Row 1: Knit 2, knit 2 together through the **back** legs, yarn over forward (i.e., from yourself), knit 2 together through the **back** legs, *yarn over forward, knit 1, yarn over forward, knit 2, knit 2 together through the **back** legs as follows: slip the 1st stitch onto the right needle purlwise, turn the next 1 clockwise twice as follows: insert the right needle through the back leg from back to front and slip it onto the right needle, thus moving the back leg to the front, return it onto the left one (now the back leg becomes the front one), then insert the right needle through the back leg and slip it onto the right needle 1 more time, return both stitches from the right needle to the left one, now knit 2 together through the **back** legs (**note:** this method of knitting 2 together makes the front stitch more even),

knit the next 4, knit the next 2 together through the **front** legs as follows: insert the right needle through the back leg of the 1st stitch from back to front and slip it onto the right needle, thus moving the back leg to the front, return it onto the left needle, insert the right needle through the back leg 1 more time and slip it onto the right needle, thus moving the back leg to the front 1 more time, leave it on the right needle, then insert the right needle through the back leg of the 2nd stitch from back to front and slip it onto the right needle, thus moving the back leg of the 2nd stitch to the front, return both stitches onto the left needle, now knit 2 together through the **front** legs (**note:** this method of knitting 2 together makes the front stitch more even), knit the next 2, yarn over forward, knit 2 together through the **back** legs* repeat from * to * until the end of the row before the edge stitch, yarn over forward, knit 2.

Row 2: Purl all the stitches.

Row 3: Knit 1, knit 2 together through the **back** legs, yarn over forward, knit 2 together through the **back** legs, yarn over forward, *knit 3, yarn over forward, knit 2, knit 2 together through the **back** legs as described in row 1, knit 2, knit 2 together through the **front** legs as described in row 1, knit 2, yarn over forward, knit 2 together through the **back** legs, yarn over forward* repeat from * to * until the end of the row before the edge stitch, knit 3.

Row 4: Purl all the stitches.

Row 5: Knit 2 together through the **back** legs, yarn over forward, knit 2 together through the **back** legs, yarn over forward, knit 1, *knit 4, yarn over forward, knit 2, knit 2 together through the **back** legs as described in row 1, knit 2 together through the **front** legs as described in row 1, knit 2, yarn over forward, knit 2 together through the **back** legs, yarn over forward, knit 1* repeat from * to * until the end of the row before the edge stitch, knit 3.

Row 6: Purl all the stitches.

Row 7: Knit 2, yarn over forward, knit 2 together through the **front** legs (move the back legs to the front, then knit 2 together), yarn over forward, *knit 2, knit 2 together through the **back** legs as described in row 1, knit 4, knit 2 together through the **front** legs as described in row 1, knit 2, yarn over forward, knit 1, yarn over forward, knit 2 together through the **front** legs (move the back legs to the front, then knit 2 together), yarn over forward* repeat from * to * until the end of the row before the edge stitch—the last 4—knit 2 together through the **front** legs (move the back legs to the front, then knit 2 together), knit 2.

Row 8: Purl all the stitches.

Row 9: Knit 3, yarn over forward, knit 2 together through the **front** legs (move the back legs to the front, then knit 2 together), *yarn over forward, knit 2, knit 2 together through the **back** legs as described in row 1, knit 2, knit 2 together through the **front** legs as described in row 1, knit 2, yarn over forward, knit 3, yarn over forward, knit 2 together through the **front** legs (move the back legs to the front, then knit 2 together)* repeat from * to * until the end of the row before the edge stitch, yarn over forward, knit 2 together through the **front** legs (move the back legs to the front, then knit 2 together), knit 1.

Row 10: Purl all the stitches.

Row 11: Knit 4, yarn over forward, *knit 2 together through the **front** legs, yarn over forward, knit 2, knit 2 together through the **back** legs as described in row 1, knit 2 together through the **front** legs as described in row 1, knit 2, yarn over forward, knit 5, yarn over forward* repeat from * to * until the end of the row before the edge stitch—the last 4—knit 2 together through the **front** legs (move the back legs to the front, then knit 2 together), yarn over forward, knit 2 together through the **front** legs (move the back legs to the front, then knit 2 together).

Row 12: Purl all the stitches.

Repeat rows: 1-12.

Bind off after the last row 12 as follows: Slip the edge stitch onto the right needle, knit the next 1, then insert the left needle through the slipped edge stitch, from left to right, and pass it over the knitted stitch, *now there is 1 stitch on the right needle, knit the next 1 (now there are 2 stitches on the right needle), insert the left needle through the 1st stitch on the right needle from left to right and pass it over the 2nd one* repeat from * to * until the end of the row.

Pattern 22

Cast on a multiple of 13, plus 19 and 2 edge stitches. Thirteen-stitch repeat. Repeat rows: 1-12. **The edge stitches are not included in the description below and must be added. Slip the first edge stitch, purl the last one.**

Knit through the back leg; purl as follows: with the working yarn in front of the stitch, insert the right needle through the stitch from back to front, move the working yarn under the right needle and pull it with the needle through the stitch. The purl stitch that works this way sets up the knit stitch for knitting through the back leg. **Needles: 2 mm.**

Description:

Row 1: Knit 2, knit the next 2 together through the **front** legs as follows: turn the 1st stitch clockwise twice as follows: insert the right needle through the back leg from back to front and slip it onto the right needle, thus moving the back leg to the front, return it onto the left needle (now the former back leg becomes the front one), insert the right needle through the back leg 1 more time and slip it onto the right needle, thus moving the back leg to the front 1 more time, leave it on the right needle, then insert the right needle through the back leg of the 2nd stitch from back to front and slip it onto the right needle, thus moving the back leg to the front, return both stitches onto the left needle, now knit 2 together through the **front** legs (**note:** this method of knitting 2 together makes the front stitch more even),then yarn over forward (i.e., from yourself), knit 1, yarn over forward, knit 2, knit the next 2 together through the **back** legs as follows: slip the 1st stitch onto the right needle purlwise, turn the next 1 clockwise twice on the left needle as follows: insert the right needle through the back leg from back to front and slip it onto the right needle, thus moving the back leg to the front, return it onto the left needle (now the former back leg becomes the front one), insert the right needle through the back leg 1 more time and slip it onto the right needle, thus moving the back leg to the front 1 more time, return both stitches from the right needle to the left one, now knit 2 together through the **back** legs (**note:** this method of knitting 2 together makes the front stitch more even), knit the next 2, *knit 2, knit the next 2 together through the **front** legs as described in this row above, knit the next 2, yarn over forward, knit 1, yarn over forward, knit 2, knit the next 2 together through the **back** legs as described in this row above, knit 2* repeat from * to * until the end of the row before the edge stitch—the last 8— knit 2, knit the next 2 together through the **front** legs as described in this row above, knit the next 2, yarn over forward, knit 2.

Row 2: Purl all the stitches.

Row 3: Knit 1, knit 2 together through the **front** legs as described in row 1, yarn over forward, knit 3, yarn over forward, knit 2, knit 2 together through the **back** legs as described in row 1, knit 1, *knit 1, knit 2 together through the **front** legs as described in row 1, knit the next 2, yarn over forward, knit 3, yarn over forward, knit 2, knit 2 together through the **back** legs as described in row 1, knit 1* repeat from * to * until the end of the row before the edge stitch—the last 8—knit 1, knit 2 together through the **front** legs as described in row 1, knit the next 2, yarn over forward, knit 3.

Row 4: Purl all the stitches.

Row 5: Knit 2 together through the **front** legs as described in row 1, yarn over forward, knit 5, yarn over forward, knit 2, knit 2 together through the **back** legs as described in row 1, *knit 2 together through the **front** legs as described in row 1, knit 2, yarn over forward, knit 5, yarn over forward, knit 2, knit 2 together through the **back**

legs as described in row 1* repeat from * to * until the end of the row before the edge stitch—the last 8--knit 2 together through the **front** legs as described in row 1, knit 2, yarn over forward, knit 4.

Row 6: Purl all the stitches.

Row 7: Knit 2, yarn over forward, knit 2, knit the next 2 together through the **back** legs as described in row 1, knit 4, knit 2 together through the **front** legs as described in row 1, *knit 2, yarn over forward, knit 1, yarn over forward, knit 2, knit 2 together through the **back** legs as described in row 1, knit 4, knit 2 together through the **front** legs as described in row 1* repeat from * to * until the end of the row before the edge stitch—the last 8—knit 2, yarn over forward, knit 1, yarn over forward, knit 2 together through the **back** legs as described in row 1, knit 2.

Row 8: Purl all the stitches.

Row 9: Knit 3, yarn over forward, knit 2, knit 2 together through the **back** legs as described in row 1, knit 2, knit 2 together through the **front** legs as described in row 1, knit 1, *knit 1, yarn over forward, knit 3, yarn over forward, knit 2, knit 2 together through the **back** legs as described in row 1, knit the next 2, knit 2 together through the **front** legs as described in row 1, knit 1* repeat from * to * until the end of the row before the edge stitch—the last 8— knit 1, yarn over forward, knit 3, yarn over forward, knit 2 together through the **back** legs as described in row 1, knit 1.

Row 10: Purl all the stitches.

Row 11: Knit 4, yarn over forward, knit 2, knit the next 2 together through the **back** legs as described in row 1, knit 2 together through the **front** legs as described in row 1, knit the next 2,
*yarn over forward, knit 5, yarn over forward, knit 2, knit 2 together through the **back** legs as described in row 1, knit 2 together through the **front** legs as described in row 1, knit 2* repeat from * to * until the end of the row before the edge stitch—the last 8—yarn over forward, knit 5, yarn over forward, knit 2 together through the **back** legs as described in row 1.

Row 12: Purl all the stitches.

Repeat rows: 1-12.

Bind off after the last row 12 as follows: Slip the edge stitch onto the right needle, knit the next 1, then insert the left needle through the slipped edge stitch, from left to right, and pass it over the knitted stitch, *now there is 1 stitch on the right needle, knit the next 1 (now there are 2 stitches on the right needle), insert the left needle through the 1st stitch on the right needle from left to right and pass it over the 2nd one* repeat from * to * until the end of the row.

Pattern 23

Cast on a multiple of 9, plus 2 and 2 edge stitches. Nine-stitch repeat. Repeat rows: 1-8.**The edge stitches are not included in the description below and must be added. Slip the first edge stitch, purl the last one.**

Knit through the back leg; purl as follows: with the working yarn in front of the stitch, insert the right needle through the stitch from back to front, move the working yarn under the right needle and pull it with the needle through the stitch. The purl stitch that works this way sets up the knit stitch for knitting through the back leg. **Needles: 2 mm.**

Description:

Row 1: Knit 2 together through the **front** legs (move the back legs to the front, then knit 2 together), *yarn over forward (i.e., from yourself), knit 3, yarn over forward, knit 1, knit 2 together through the **back** legs as follows: slip the 1st stitch onto the right needle purlwise, turn the next 1 clockwise twice on the left needle as follows: insert the right needle through the back leg from back to front and slip it onto the right needle, thus moving the back leg to the front, return it onto the left needle (now the former back leg becomes the front one), insert the right needle through the back leg 1 more time and slip it onto the right needle, thus moving the back leg to the front 1 more time, return both stitches from the right needle to the left one, now knit 2 together through the **back** legs (**note:** this method of knitting 2 together makes the front stitch more even), knit the next 2 together through the **front** legs as follows: turn the 1st stitch clockwise twice as follows: insert the right needle through the back leg from back to front and slip it onto the right needle, thus moving the back leg to the front, return it onto the left needle (now the former back leg becomes the front one), insert the right needle through the back leg 1 more time and slip it onto the right needle, thus moving the back leg to the front 1 more time, leave it on the right needle, then insert the right needle through the back leg of the 2nd stitch from back to front and slip it onto the right needle, thus moving the back leg to the front, return both stitches onto the left needle, now knit 2 together through the **front** legs (**note:** this method of knitting 2 together makes the front stitch more even), knit the next 1* repeat from * to * until the end of the row before the edge stitch, **yarn over forward** (i.e., from yourself).

Row 2: Purl all the stitches.

Row 3: Knit 1, *knit 1, knit 2 together through the **front** legs as described in row 1, knit 1, yarn over forward, knit 1, yarn over forward, knit 1, knit 2 together through the **back** legs as described in row 1, knit 1* repeat from * to * until the end of the row before the edge stitch, knit 1.

Row 4: Purl all the stitches.

Row 5: Knit 1, *knit 2 together through the **front** legs as described in row 1, knit 1, yarn over forward, knit 3, yarn over forward, knit 1, knit 2 together through the **back** legs as described in row 1* repeat from * to * until the end of the row before the edge stitch, knit 1.

Row 6: Purl all the stitches.

Row 7: Knit 2 together through the **front** legs as described in row 1, *knit 1, yarn over forward, knit 1, yarn over forward, knit 1, knit 2 together through the **back** legs as described in row 1, knit the next 2, knit the next 2 together through the **front** legs as described in row 1* repeat from * to * until the end of the row before the edge stitch, **yarn over forward.**

Row 8: Purl all the stitches.

Repeat rows: 1-8.

Bind off after the last row 8 as follows: Slip the edge stitch onto the right needle, knit the next 1, then insert the left needle through the slipped edge stitch, from left to right, and pass it over the knitted stitch, *now there is 1 stitch on the right needle, knit the next 1 (now there are 2 stitches on the right needle), insert the left needle through the 1st stitch on the right needle, from left to right, and pass it over the 2nd one* repeat from * to * until the end of the row.

Pattern 24

Option 1

Cast on a multiple of 3, plus 2 edge stitches. Three-stitch repeat. Repeat rows: 1-4.**The edge stitches are not included in the description below and must be added. Slip the first edge stitch, purl the last one as follows:** with the working yarn in front of the stitch, insert the right needle through the stitch from back to front, move the working yarn under the right needle and pull it with the needle through the stitch.

Pattern 25

Option 1

Cast on a multiple of 11, plus 2 edge stitches. Eleven-stitch repeat. Repeat rows: 1-8.**The edge stitches are not included in the description below and must be added. Slip the first edge stitch, purl the last one.**

Knit through the back leg, purl as follows: with the working yarn in front of the stitch, insert the right needle through the stitch from back to front, move the working yarn under the right needle and pull it with the needle through the stitch. The purl stitch that works this way sets up the knit stitch for knitting through the back leg. **Needles: 2.5 mm.**

Description:

Row 1: *Knit 2 together through the **front** legs as follows: slip the 1st stitch onto the right needle purlwise, slip the 2nd stitch onto the right needle as follows: insert the right needle through the back leg from back to front, thus moving the back leg to the front, return both stitches onto the left needle, now knit 2 together through the **front** legs, then knit the next 2, yarn over forward (i.e., from yourself), knit 1, yarn over forward, knit 2, knit 2 together through the **back** legs as follows: slip the 1st stitch onto the right needle purlwise, slip the 2nd stitch onto the right needle, inserting the right needle through the back leg from back to front, thus moving the back leg to the front, return both stitches onto the left needle, now knit 2 together through the **back** legs, then knit the next 2* repeat from * to * until the end of the row.

Row 2: Purl all the stitches.

Row 3: *Knit 6, yarn over forward, knit 2, knit 2 together through the **back** legs as described in row 1, knit 1* repeat from * to * until the end of the row.

Row 4: Purl all the stitches.

Row 5: *Knit 2, knit 2 together through the **front** legs as described in row 1, knit 2, yarn over forward, knit 1, yarn over forward, knit 2, knit 2 together through the **back** legs as described in row 1* repeat from * to * until the end of the row.

Row 6: Purl all the stitches.

Row 7: *Knit 1, knit 2 together through the **front** legs as described in row 1, knit 2, yarn over forward, knit 6* repeat from * to * until the end of the row.

Row 8: Purl all the stitches.

Repeat rows: 1-8.

Bind off after the last row 8 as follows: Slip the edge stitch onto the right needle, knit the next 1, then insert the left needle through the slipped edge stitch, from left to right, and pass it over the knitted stitch, *now there is 1 stitch on the right needle, knit the next 1 (now there are 2 stitches on the right needle), insert the left needle through the 1st stitch on the right needle, from left to right, and pass it over the 2nd one* repeat from * to * until the end of the row.

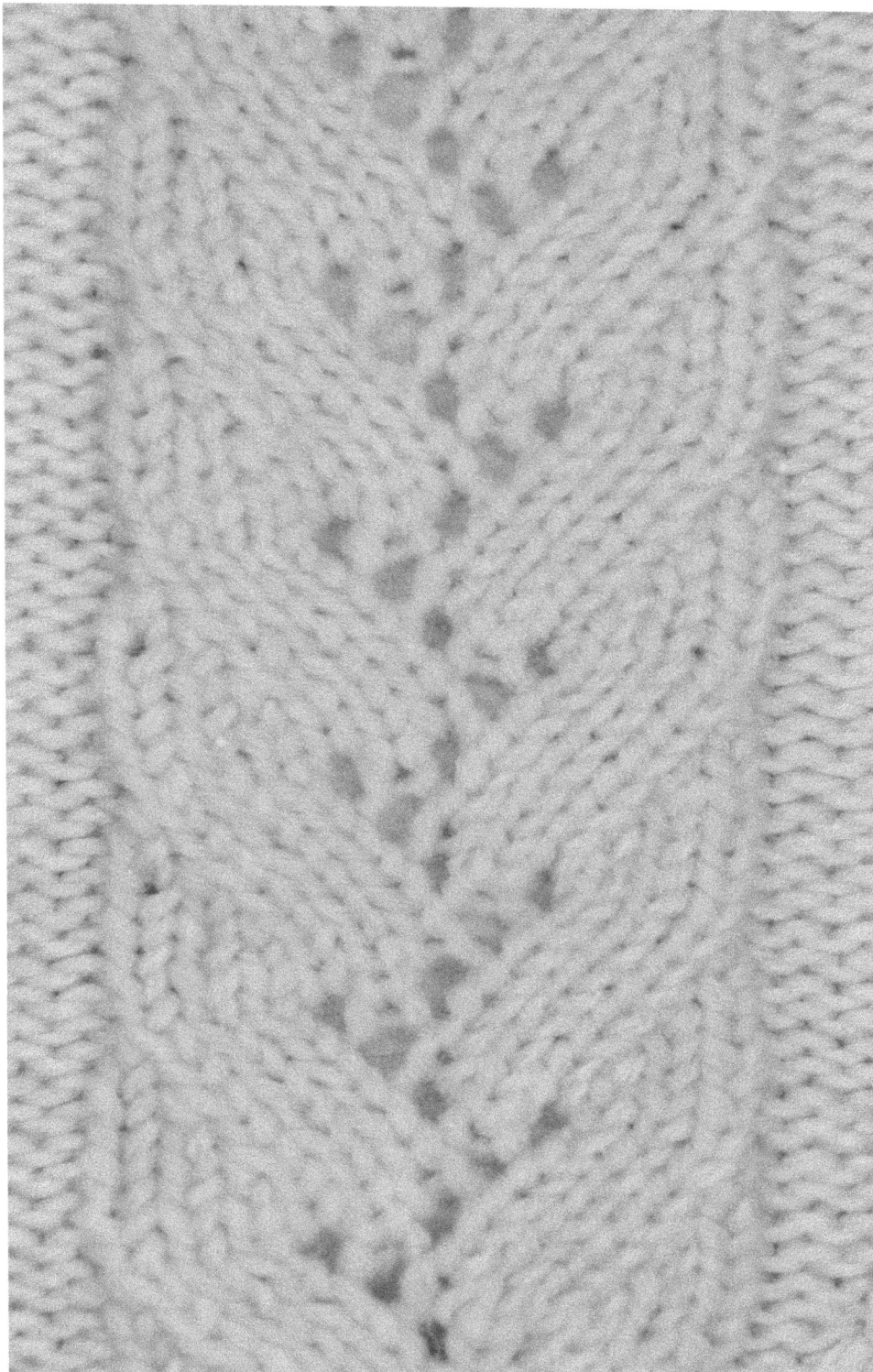

Cast on 11 stitches for the braid; the number of adjacent stitches is optional. Knit from * to * as described above.

Pattern 26

Cast on a multiple of 24, plus 2 edge stitches. Twenty-four-stitch repeat. Repeat rows: 1-24. **The edge stitches are not included in the description below and must be added. Slip the first edge stitch, purl the last one.**

72

Knit through the back leg; purl as follows: with the working yarn in front of the stitch, insert the right needle through the stitch from back to front, move the working yarn under the right needle and pull it with the needle through the stitch. The purl stitch that works this way sets up the knit stitch for knitting through the back leg. **Needles: 2.5 mm.**

Description:

Row 1: *Knit 4, knit 2 together through the **front** legs as follows: insert the right needle through the back leg of the 1st stitch from back to front and slip it onto the right needle, thus moving the back leg to the front, return it onto the left one, thus the back leg becomes the front one, insert the right needle through the back leg from back to front 1 more time and slip it onto the right needle 1 more time, leave it on the right needle, then insert the right needle through the back leg of the 2nd stitch from back to front and slip it onto the right needle, thus moving the back leg of the 2nd stitch to the front, return both stitches onto the left needle, now knit 2 together through the **front** legs (**note:** this method of knitting 2 together makes the front stitch more even), knit the next 2, yarn over forward (i.e., from yourself), knit 5, yarn over forward, knit 2, knit 2 together through the **back** legs as follows: slip the 1st stitch onto the right needle purlwise, turn the 2nd one clockwise twice as follows: insert the right needle through the back leg from back to front and slip it onto the right needle, thus moving the back leg to the front, return it onto the left needle, then insert the right needle through the back leg from back to front 1 more time and slip it onto the right needle 1 more time, return both stitches onto the left needle, now knit 2 together through the **back** legs (**note:** this method of knitting 2 together makes the front stitch more even), then knit 2, yarn over forward, knit 2, knit the next 2 together through the **back** legs as described in this row above, knit 1* repeat from * to * until the end of the row.

Row 2: Purl all the stitches.

Row 3: *Knit 3, knit 2 together through the **front** legs as described in row 1, knit the next 2, yarn over forward, knit 2, knit 2 together through the **front** legs as described in row 1, knit 2, yarn over forward, knit 1, yarn over forward, knit 2, knit 2 together through the **back** legs as described in row 1, knit 2, yarn over forward, knit 2, knit 2 together through the **back** legs as described in row 1* repeat from * to * until the end of the row.

Row 4: Purl all the stitches.

Row 5: *Knit 2, knit 2 together through the **front** legs as described in row 1, knit 2, yarn over forward, knit 2, knit 2 together through the **front** legs as described in row 1, knit 2, yarn over forward, knit 3, yarn over forward, knit 2, knit 2 together through the **back** legs as described in row 1, knit 5* repeat from * to * until the end of the row.

Row 6: Purl all the stitches.

Row 7: *Knit 1, knit 2 together through the **front** legs as described in row 1, knit 2, yarn over forward, knit 2, knit 2 together through the **front** legs as described in row 1, knit 2, yarn over forward, knit 5, yarn over forward, knit 2, knit 2 together through the **back** legs as described in row 1, knit 4* repeat from * to * until the end of the row.

Row 8: Purl all the stitches.

Row 9: *Knit 2 together through the **front** legs as described in row 1, knit 2, yarn over forward, knit 2, knit 2 together through the **front** legs as described in row 1, knit 2, yarn over forward, knit 1, yarn over forward, knit 2, knit 2 together through the **back** legs as described in row 1, knit 2, yarn over forward, knit 2, knit 2 together through the **back** legs as described in row 1, knit 3* repeat from * to * until the end of the row.

Row 10: Purl all the stitches.

Row 11: *Knit 5, knit the next 2 together through the **front** legs as described in row 1, knit 2, yarn over forward, knit 3, yarn over forward, knit 2, knit 2 together through the **back** legs as described in row 1, knit 2, yarn over forward, knit 2, knit 2 together through the **back** legs as described in row 1, knit 2* repeat from * to * until the end of the row.

Row 12: Purl all the stitches.

Row 13: *Knit 4, knit 2 together through the **front** legs as described in row 1, knit the next 2, yarn over forward, knit 5, yarn over forward, knit 2, knit 2 together through the **back** legs as described in row 1, knit 2, yarn over forward, knit 2, knit 2 together through the **back** legs as described in row 1, knit 1* repeat from * to * until the end of the row.

Row 14: Purl all the stitches.

Row 15: *Knit 3, knit 2 together through the **front** legs as described in row 1, knit 2, yarn over forward, knit 2, knit 2 together through the **front** legs as described in row 1, knit 2, yarn over forward, knit 1, yarn over forward, knit 2, knit 2 together through the **back** legs as described in row 1, knit 2, yarn over forward, knit 2, knit 2 together through the **back** legs as described in row 1* repeat from * to * until the end of the row.

Row 16: Purl all the stitches.

Row 17: *Knit 2, knit 2 together through the **front** legs as described in row 1, knit 2, yarn over forward, knit 2, knit 2 together through the **front** legs as described in row 1, knit 2, yarn over forward, knit 3, yarn over forward, knit 2, knit 2 together through the **back** legs as described in row 1, knit 5* repeat from * to * until the end of the row.

Row 18: Purl all the stitches.

Row 19: *Knit 1, knit 2 together through the **front** legs as described in row 1, knit 2, yarn over forward, knit 2, knit 2 together through the **front** legs as described in row 1, knit 2, yarn over forward, knit 5, yarn over forward, knit 2, knit 2 together through the **back** legs as described in row 1, knit 4* repeat from * to * until the end of the row.

Row 20: Purl all the stitches.

Row 21: *Knit 2 together through the **front** legs as described in row 1, knit 2, yarn over forward, knit 2, knit 2 together through the **front** legs as described in row 1, knit 2, yarn over forward, knit 1, yarn over forward, knit 2, knit 2 together through the **back** legs as described in row 1, knit 2, yarn over forward, knit 2, knit 2 together through the **back** legs as described in row 1, knit 3* repeat from * to * until the end of the row.

74

Row 22: Purl all the stitches.

Row 23: *Knit 5, knit the next 2 together through the **front** legs as described in row 1, knit 2, yarn over forward, knit 3, yarn over forward, knit 2, knit 2 together through the **back** legs as described in row 1, knit 2, yarn over forward, knit 2, knit 2 together through the **back** legs as described in row 1, knit 2* repeat from * to * until the end of the row.

Row 24: Purl all the stitches.

Repeat rows: 1-24.

Bind off after the last row 24 as follows: Slip the edge stitch onto the right needle, knit the next 1, then insert the left needle through the slipped edge stitch, from left to right, and pass it over the knitted stitch, *now there is 1 stitch on the right needle, knit the next 1 (now there are 2 stitches on the right needle), insert the left needle through the 1st stitch on the right needle, from left to right, and pass it over the 2nd one* repeat from * to * until the end of the row.

Option 2

Center braid. Knit the same as described in option 1.

Pattern 27

Option 1

Cast on a multiple of 16, plus 2 edge stitches. Sixteen-stitch repeat. Repeat rows: 1-12. **The edge stitches are not included in the description below and must be added. Slip the first edge stitch, purl the last one.**

Knit through the back leg; purl as follows: with the working yarn in front of the stitch, insert the right needle through the stitch from back to front, move the working yarn under the right needle and pull it with the needle through the stitch. The purl stitch that works this way sets up the knit stitch for knitting through the back leg. **Needles: 2.5 mm.**

Description:

Row 1: *Knit 3, knit 2 together through the **front** legs as follows: insert the right needle through the back leg of the 1st stitch from back to front and slip it onto the right needle, thus moving the back leg to the front, return it onto the left one, thus the back leg becomes the front one, then insert the right needle through the back leg from back to front and slip it onto the right needle 1 more time, thus moving the back leg to the front 1 more time, leave it on the right needle, then insert the right needle through the back leg of the 2nd stitch from back to front and slip it onto the right needle, thus moving the back leg of the 2nd stitch to the front, return both stitches onto the left needle, now knit 2 together through the **front** legs (**note:** this method of knitting 2 together makes the front stitch more even), then knit the next 2, yarn over forward (i.e., from yourself), knit 5, yarn over forward, knit 2, knit the next 2 together through the **back** legs as follows: slip the 1st stitch onto the right needle purlwise, turn the 2nd stitch clockwise twice as follows: insert the right needle through the back leg from back to front and slip it onto the right needle, thus moving the back leg to the front, return it onto the left one, thus the back leg becomes the front one, insert the right needle through the back leg from back to front and slip it onto the right needle, thus moving the back leg to the front 1 more time, return both stitches onto the left needle, now knit 2 together through the **back** legs (**note:** this method of knitting 2 together makes the front stitch more even)* repeat from * to * until the end of the row.

Row 2: Purl all the stitches.

Row 3: *Knit 2, knit 2 together through the **front** legs as described in row 1, knit the next 2, yarn over forward, knit 1, yarn over forward, knit 2, knit 2 together through the **back** legs as described in row 1, knit 5* repeat from * to * until the end of the row.

Row 4: Purl all the stitches.

Row 5: *Knit 1, knit 2 together through the **front** legs as described in row 1, knit the next 2, yarn over forward, knit 3, yarn over forward, knit 2, knit 2 together through the **back** legs as described in row 1, knit 4* repeat from * to * until the end of the row.

Row 6: Purl all the stitches.

Row 7: *Knit 2 together through the **front** legs as described in row 1, knit the next 2, yarn over forward (i.e., from yourself), knit 5, yarn over forward, knit 2, knit the next 2 together through the **back** legs as described in row 1, knit 3* repeat from * to * until the end of the row.

Row 8: Purl all the stitches.

Option 2

Knit the braid from * to *as described in option 1; the number of adjacent stitches is optional.

Pattern 29

Cast on a multiple of 16, plus 1 for symmetry and 2 edge stitches. Sixteen-stitch repeat. Repeat rows: 1-8. **The edge stitches are not included in the description below and must be added. Slip the first edge stitch, purl the last one.**

Knit through the back leg; purl as follows: with the working yarn in front of the stitch, insert the right needle through the stitch from back to front, move the working yarn under the right needle and pull it with the needle through the stitch. The purl stitch that works this way sets up the knit stitch for knitting through the back leg. **Needles: 2.5 mm.**

Description:

Row 1: *Purl 1, knit 2 together through the **front** legs as follows: insert the right needle through the back leg of the 1st stitch from back to front and slip it onto the right needle, thus moving the back leg to the front, return it onto the left one, now the back leg becomes the front one, then insert the right needle through the back leg from back to front and slip it onto the right needle 1 more time, thus moving the back leg to the front 1 more time, leave it on the right needle, then insert the right needle through the back leg of the 2nd stitch from back to front and slip it onto the right needle, thus moving the back leg of the 2nd stitch to the front, return both stitches onto the left needle, now knit 2 together through the **front** legs, then knit the next 1, yarn over forward (i.e., from yourself), knit 1, knit 2 together through the **front** legs as described above, knit 1, yarn over forward, knit 1, yarn over forward, knit 1, knit the next 2 together through the **back** legs as follows: slip the 1st stitch onto the right needle purlwise, turn the 2nd stitch clockwise twice as follows: insert the right needle through the back leg from back to front and slip it onto the right needle, thus moving the back leg to the front, return it onto the left one, now the back leg becomes the front one, then insert the right needle through the back leg from back to front 1 more time and slip it onto the right needle, thus moving the back leg to the front 1 more time, return both stitches onto the left needle, now knit 2 together through the **back** legs, then knit 1, yarn over forward, knit 1, knit the next 2 together through the **back** legs as described in this row above* repeat from * to * until the end of the row before the edge stitch, purl 1.

Row 2: *Knit 1, purl 15* repeat from * to * until the end of the row before the edge stitch, knit 1.

Row 3: *Purl 1, yarn over forward, knit 2 together through the **back** legs as described in row 1, knit the next 1, knit 2 together through the **front** legs as described in row 1, knit 1, yarn over forward, knit 3, yarn over forward, knit 1, knit 2 together through the **back** legs as described in row 1, knit 1, knit 2 together through the **front** legs as described in row 1, yarn over forward* repeat from * to * until the end of the row before the edge stitch, purl 1.

Row 4: *Knit 1, purl 15* repeat from * to * until the end of the row before the edge stitch, knit 1.

Row 5: *Purl 1, purl 1 through the back leg, yarn over forward, knit 3 together through the **front** legs as described in row 1, except the following: turn the first 2 stitches clockwise twice before knitting, instead of turning only the 1st stitch, knit the next 1, yarn over forward, knit 5, yarn over forward, knit 1, knit 3 together through the **back** legs as described in row 1, except the following: turn the first 2 stitches clockwise twice, instead of 1, yarn over forward, purl 1 through the back leg* repeat from * to * until the end of the row before the edge stitch, purl 1.

Row 6: *Knit 2, purl 13, knit 1* repeat from * to * until the end of the row before the edge stitch, knit 1.

Row 7: *Purl 2, Knit 2 together through the **front** legs as described in row 1, knit the next 1, yarn over forward (i.e., from yourself), knit 7, yarn over forward, knit 1, knit the next 2 together through the **back** legs as described in row 1, purl 1* repeat from * to * until the end of the row before the edge stitch, purl 1.

Row 8: *Knit 2, purl 13, knit 1* repeat from * to * until the end of the row before the edge stitch, knit 1.

Repeat rows: 1-8.

Bind off after the last row 8 as follows: Slip the edge stitch onto the right needle, knit the next 1, then insert the left needle through the slipped edge stitch, from left to right, and pass it over the knitted stitch, *now there is 1 stitch on the right needle, knit the next 1 (now there are 2 stitches on the right needle), insert the left needle through the 1st stitch on the right needle, from left to right, and pass it over the 2nd one* repeat from * to * until the end of the row.

Pattern 30

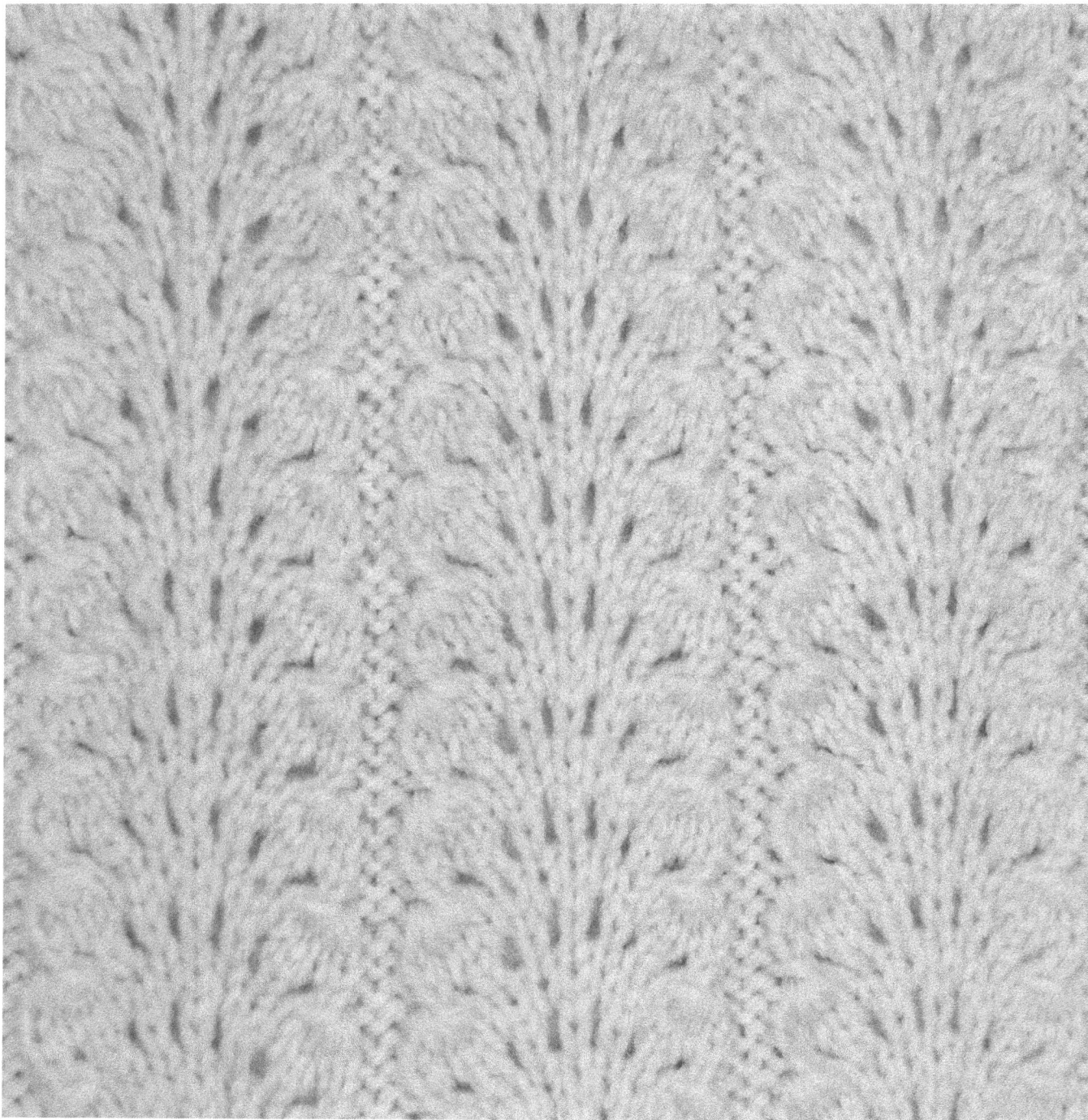

Cast on a multiple of 15, plus 2 for symmetry and 2 edge stitches. Fifteen-stitch repeat. Repeat rows: 1-4. **The edge stitches are not included in the description below and must be added. Slip the first edge stitch, purl as follows:** with the working yarn in front of the stitch, insert the right needle through the stitch from back to front, move the working yarn under the right needle and pull it with the needle through the stitch.

Knit through the front leg; purl as follows: with the working yarn in front of the stitch, insert the right needle through the stitch from back to front, wrap the working yarn counterclockwise around the tip of the right needle, then pull it with the needle through the stitch. The purl stitch that works this way sets up the knit stitch for knitting through the front leg. **Needles: 2.5 mm. Knit tightly.**

Description:

Row 1: *Purl 2, knit 4 together through the **front** legs, yarn over forward (i.e., from yourself), knit 1, yarn over forward, knit 1, yarn over forward, knit 1, yarn over forward, knit 1, yarn over forward, knit 1, then make 1 more yarn over forward, knit the next 4 together through the **back** legs as follows: insert the right needle through the 1st stitch on the left needle from front to back and slip it onto the right needle, repeat 3 more times, thus moving the front legs of these 4 stitches to the back, return these 4 stitches onto the left needle, now knit 4 together through the **back** legs* repeat from * to * until the end of the row before the edge stitch, purl 2.

Row 2: *Knit 2, purl 13* repeat from * to * until the end of the row before the edge stitch, knit 2.

Row 3: *Purl 2, knit 13* repeat from * to * until the end of the row before the edge stitch, purl 2.

Row 4: *Knit 2, purl 13* repeat from * to * until the end of the row before the edge stitch, knit 2.

Repeat rows: 1-4.

Bind off after the last row 4 as follows: Slip the edge stitch onto the right needle, knit the next 1, then insert the left needle through the slipped edge stitch, from left to right, and pass it over the knitted stitch, *now there is 1 stitch on the right needle, knit the next 1 (now there are 2 stitches on the right needle), insert the left needle through the 1st stitch on the right needle, from left to right, and pass it over the 2nd one* repeat from * to * until the end of the row.

Pattern 31

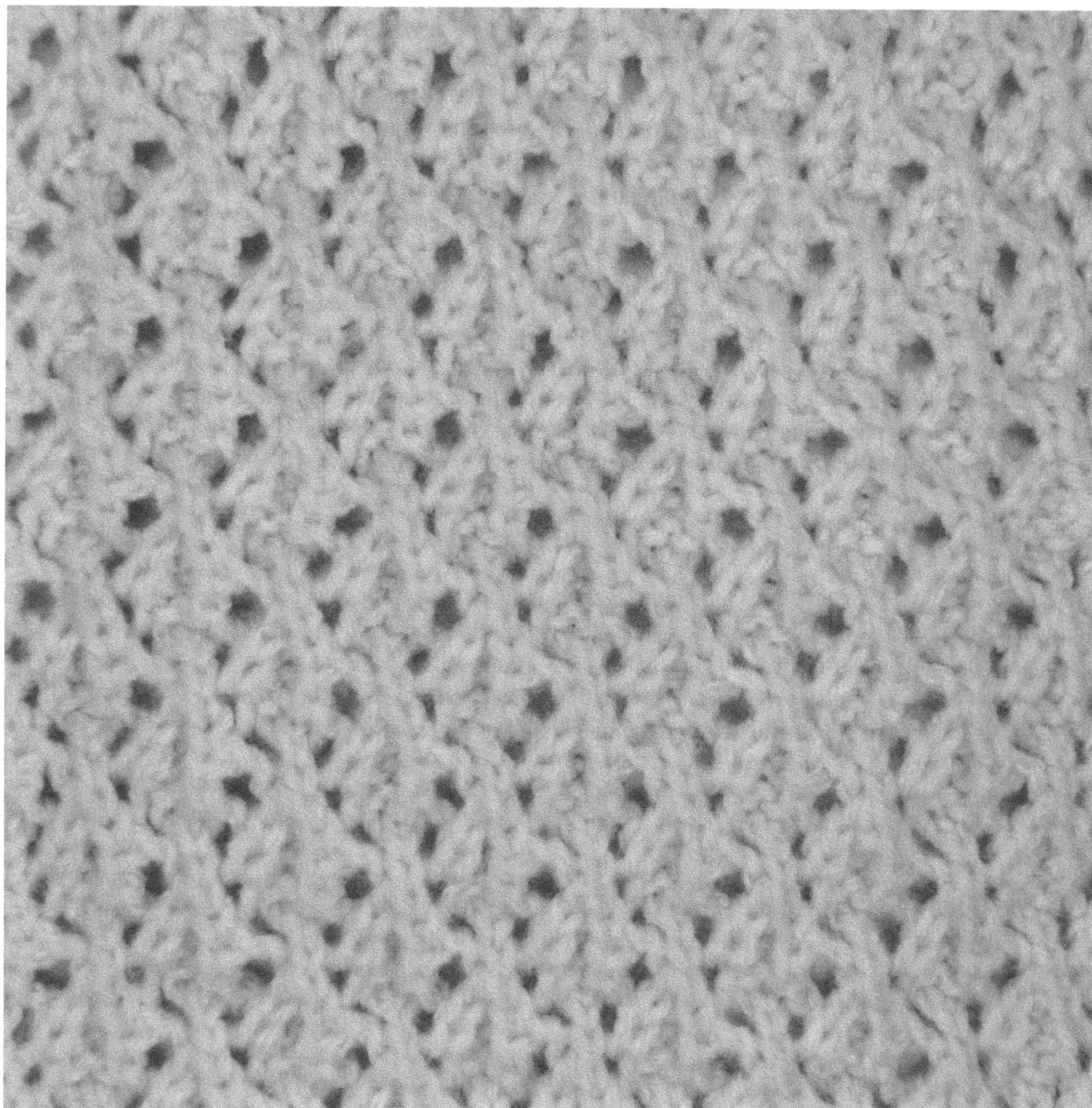

Cast on a multiple of 6, plus 7 and 2 edge stitches. Six-stitch repeat. Repeat rows: 1-8. **The edge stitches are not included in the description below and must be added. Slip the first edge stitch, purl as follows:** with the working yarn in front of the stitch, insert the right needle through the stitch from back to front, move the working yarn under the right needle and pull it with the needle through the stitch.

Knit through the front leg; purl as follows: with the working yarn in front of the stitch, insert the right needle through the stitch from back to front, wrap the working yarn counterclockwise around the tip of the right needle, then pull it with the needle through the stitch. The purl stitch that works this way sets up the knit stitch for knitting through the front leg. **Needles: 2.5 mm. Knit tightly.**

Description:

Row 1: Purl 2, *yarn over forward (i.e., from yourself), knit 3 together through the **back** legs as follows: slip 1 onto the right needle, inserting the right needle from front to back, thus moving the front leg to the back, leave this stitch on the right needle, turn the next 1 on the left needle clockwise twice as follows: insert the right needle through the back leg from back to front and slip it onto the right needle, thus moving the back leg to the front, return it from the right needle to the left one, now the back leg becomes the front one, then insert the right needle through the back leg from back to front 1 more time and slip it onto the right needle, thus moving the back leg to the front 1 more time, leave this stitch on the right needle too, then insert the right needle through the front leg of the 3rd stitch from front to back and slip it onto the right needle, thus moving the front leg to the back, return these 3 stitches onto the left needle, now knit 3 together through the **back** legs, then yarn over forward, purl 3* repeat from * to * until the end of the row before the edge stitch—the last 5 stitches—yarn over forward (i.e., from yourself), knit 3 together through the **back** legs as described in this row above, yarn over forward, purl 2.

Row 2: Knit 2, *purl 3, knit 3* repeat from * to * until the end of the row before the edge stitch, purl 3, knit 2.

Row 3: Purl 1, knit 2 together through the **front** legs, *yarn over forward, knit 1, yarn over forward, knit 2 together through the **back** legs as follows: insert the right needle through the front leg of the 1st stitch from front to back and slip it onto the right needle, thus moving the front leg to the back, insert the right needle through the 2nd stitch from front to back and slip it onto the right needle, return both stitches onto the left needle, now knit 2 together through the back legs, then purl 1, knit 2 together through the **front** leg* repeat from * to * until the end of the row before the edge stitch—the last 4 stitches—yarn over forward, knit 1, yarn over forward, knit 2 together through the **back** legs as follows: slip 1 onto the right needle, inserting the right needle from front to back, thus moving the front leg to the back, leave this stitch on the right needle, turn the next 1 on the left needle clockwise twice as follows: insert the right needle through the back leg from back to front and slip it onto the right needle, thus moving the back leg to the front, return it from the right needle to the left one, now the back leg becomes the front one, then insert the right needle through the back leg from back to front 1 more time and slip it onto the right needle, thus moving the back leg to the front 1 more time, return both stitches onto the left needle, now knit 2 together through the **back** legs, then purl 1.

Row 4: Knit 1, *purl 5, knit 1* repeat from * to * until the end of the row.

Row 5: Knit 2 together through the **front** legs, yarn over forward, *purl 3, yarn over forward, knit 3 together through the **back** legs as follows as described in row 1, yarn over forward* repeat from * to * until the end of the row before the edge stitch—the last 5 stitches—purl 3, yarn over forward, knit 2 together through the **back** legs as described in row 3.

Row 6: Purl 2, *knit 3, purl 3* repeat from * to * until the end of the row before the edge stitch, knit 3, purl 2.

Row 7: Knit 1, yarn over forward, *knit 2 together through the **back** legs as described in row 3, purl 1, knit 2 together through the **front** legs, yarn over forward, knit 1, yarn over forward* repeat from * to * until the end of the row before the edge stitch—the last 6 stitches—knit 2 together through the **back** legs as described in row 3, purl 1, knit 2 together through the **front** legs, yarn over forward, knit 1.

Row 8: Purl 3, *knit 1, purl 5* repeat from * to * until the end of the row before the edge stitch, knit 1, purl 3.

Repeat rows: 1-8.

Bind off after the last row 8 as follows: Slip the edge stitch onto the right needle, knit the next 1, then insert the left needle through the slipped edge stitch, from left to right, and pass it over the knitted stitch, *now there is 1 stitch on the right needle, knit the next 1 (now there are 2 stitches on the right needle), insert the left needle through the 1st stitch on the right needle, from left to right, and pass it over the 2nd one* repeat from * to * until the end of the row.

Pattern 32

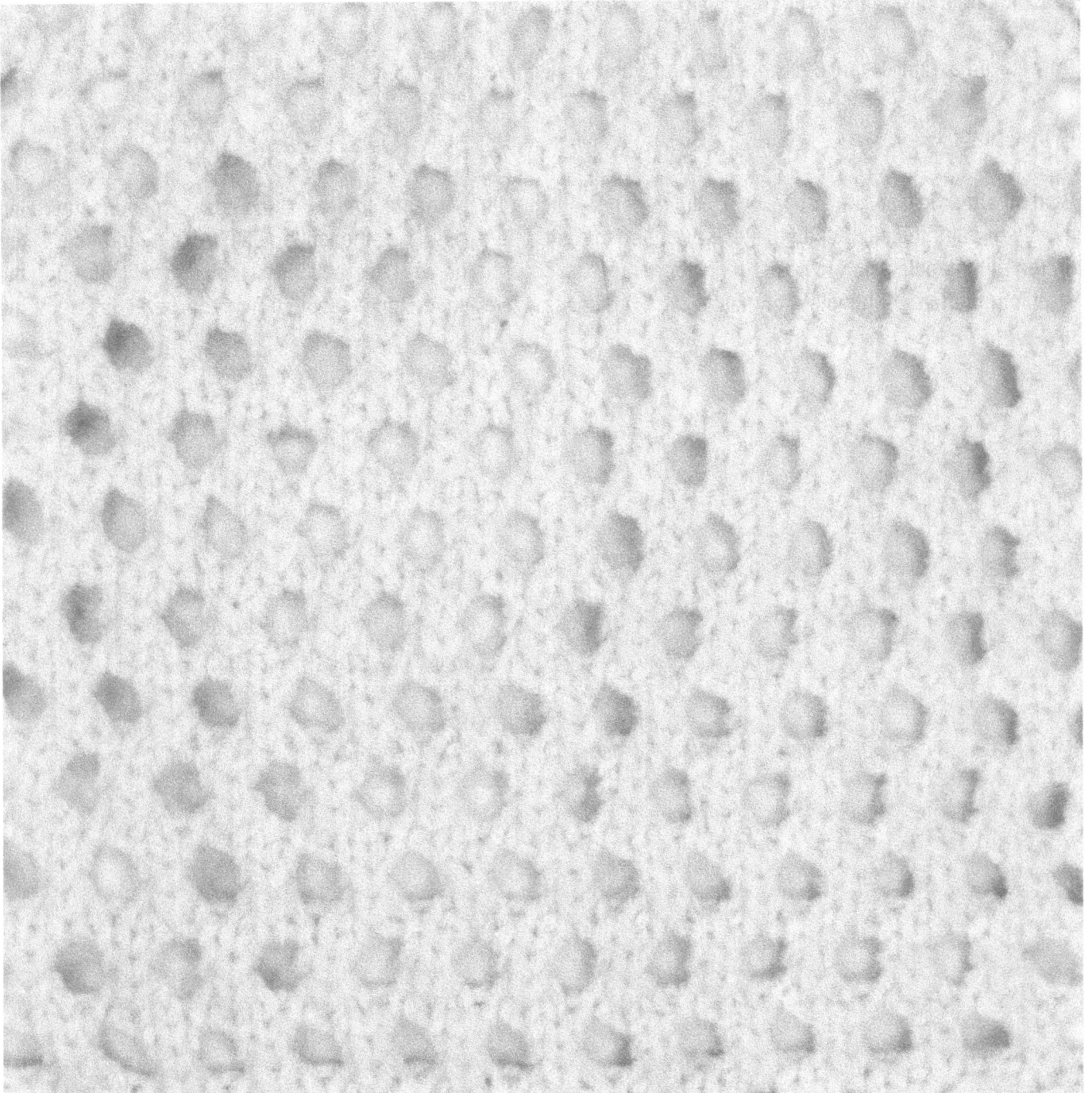

Cast on a multiple of 3, plus 1 and 2 edge stitches. Three-stitch repeat. Repeat rows: 1-8. **The edge stitches are not included in the description below and must be added. Slip the first edge stitch, purl as follows:** with the working yarn in front of the stitch, insert the right needle through the stitch from back to front, move the working yarn under the right needle and pull it with the needle through the stitch.

Knit through the front leg; purl as follows: with the working yarn in front of the stitch, insert the right needle through the stitch from back to front, wrap the working yarn counterclockwise around the tip of the right needle, then pull it with the needle through the stitch. The purl stitch that works this way sets up the knit stitch for knitting through the front leg. **Needles: 2.5 mm.**

Description:

Row 1: *Knit 3 together through the **back** legs as follows: slip 2 onto the right needle knitwise, i.e., inserting the right needle through both stitches simultaneously from left to right, i.e., through the 2nd stitch then through the 1st one, thus moving the front legs to the back, now the 2nd stitch becomes the 1st one, slip the 3rd stitch onto the right needle knitwise, inserting the right needle from left to right, thus moving the front leg to the back, return these 3 stitches onto the left needle, now knit 3 together through the **back** legs, then yarn over forward (i.e., from yourself) twice* repeat from * to * until the end of the row before the edge stitch, knit 1.

Row 2: *Purl 2 (the 2nd stitch is the 1st former yarn over of the previous row), slip the next 1 off the left needle and leave it as is (the 2nd former yarn over of the previous row)* repeat from * to * until the end of the row before the edge stitch, purl 1.

Row 3: *Knit 2, make 1 as follows: with the working yarn behind your work, insert the right needle from front to back 1 row below, i.e., through the hole of the previous row, and pull the working yarn onto the right needle* repeat from * to * until the end of the row before the edge stitch, knit 1.

Row 4: Purl all the stitches.

Row 5: Knit 1, *yarn over forward twice, knit 3 together through the **back** legs as described in row 1* repeat from * to * until the end of the row.

Row 6: *Purl 2 (the 2nd stitch is the 1st former yarn over of the previous row), slip the next 1 off the left needle and leave it as is (the 2nd former yarn over of the previous row) * repeat from * to * until the end of the row before the edge stitch, purl 1.

Row 7: Knit 1, *knit 1, make 1 as follows: with the working yarn behind your work, insert the right needle from front to back 1 row below, i.e., through the hole of the previous row, and pull the working yarn onto the right needle, knit the next 1* repeat from * to * until the end of the row.

Row 8: Purl all the stitches.

Repeat rows: 1-8.

Bind off after the last row 8 as follows: Slip the edge stitch onto the right needle, knit the next 1, then insert the left needle through the slipped edge stitch, from left to right, and pass it over the knitted stitch, *now there is 1 stitch on the right needle, knit the next 1 (now there are 2 stitches on the right needle), insert the left needle through the 1st stitch on the right needle, from left to right, and pass it over the 2nd one* repeat from * to * until the end of the row.

Pattern 33

Cast on a multiple of 4, plus 2 edge stitches. Four-stitch repeat. Repeat rows: 1-8. **The edge stitches are not included in the description below and must be added. Slip the first edge stitch, purl as follows:** with the working yarn in front of the stitch, insert the right needle through the stitch from back to front, move the working yarn under the right needle and pull it with the needle through the stitch.

Knit through the front leg; purl as follows: with the working yarn in front of the stitch, insert the right needle through the stitch from back to front, wrap the working yarn counterclockwise around the tip of the right needle, then pull it with the needle through the stitch. The purl stitch that works this way sets up the knit stitch for knitting through the front leg. **Needles: 2 mm.**

Description:

Row 1: *Knit 2 together through the **front** legs as follows: insert the right needle through the 1st stitch from back to front and slip it onto the right needle, thus moving the back leg to the front, return it onto the left needle, now knit 2 together through the **front** legs, yarn over forward (i.e., from yourself) **twice**, knit 2 together through the **back** legs as follows: insert the right needle through the 1st stitch from front to back and slip it onto the right needle, thus moving the front leg to the back, leave this stitch on the right needle, insert the right needle through the 2nd stitch from back to front and slip it onto the right needle, thus moving the back leg to the front, return both stitches onto the left needle, now knit 2 together through the **back** legs* repeat from * to * until the end of the row (**note:** this method of knitting 2 together makes the front stitch more even).

Row 2: *Purl 2 (the 2nd stitch is the 1st former yarn over of the previous row), slip the next 1 off the left needle and leave it as is (the 2nd former yarn over of the previous row), purl the next 1* repeat from * to * until the end of the row.

Row 3: *Knit 2, make 1 as follows: with the working yarn behind your work, insert the right needle from front to back 1 row below, i.e., through the hole of the previous row, and pull the working yarn onto the right needle, knit the next 1* repeat from * to * until the end of the row.

Row 4: Purl all the stitches.

Row 5: Knit 2, *knit 2 together through the front legs as described in row 1, yarn over forward (i.e., from yourself) **twice**, knit 2 together through the **back** legs as described in row 1* repeat from * to * until the end of the row before the edge stitch, knit the last 2.

Row 6: Purl 2, *purl 2 (the 2nd stitch is the 1st former yarn over of the previous row), slip the next 1 off the left needle and leave it as is (the 2nd former yarn over of the previous row), purl the next 1* repeat from * to * until the end of the row before the edge stitch, purl 2.

Row 7: Knit 2, *knit 2, make 1 as follows: with the working yarn behind your work, insert the right needle from front to back 1 row below, i.e., through the hole of the previous row, and pull the working yarn onto the right needle, knit the next 1* repeat from * to * until the end of the row before the edge stitch, knit the last 2.

Row 8: Purl all the stitches.

Repeat rows: 1-8.

Bind off after the last row 8 as follows: Slip the edge stitch onto the right needle, knit the next 1, then insert the left needle through the slipped edge stitch, from left to right, and pass it over the knitted stitch, *now there is 1 stitch on the right needle, knit the next 1 (now there are 2 stitches on the right needle), insert the left needle through the 1st stitch on the right needle, from left to right, and pass it over the 2nd one* repeat from * to * until the end of the row.

Pattern 34

Cast on a multiple of 12, plus 5 and 2 edge stitches. Twelve-stitch repeat. Repeat rows: 1-26. **The edge stitches are not included in the description below and must be added. Slip the first edge stitch, purl the last one.**

Knit through the back leg, purl as follows: with the working yarn in front of the stitch, insert the right needle through the stitch from back to front, move the working yarn under the right needle and pull it with the needle through the stitch. The purl stitch that works this way sets up the knit stitch for knitting through the back leg. **Needles: 2.5 mm.**

Description:

Row 1: *Knit 10, knit 2 together through the **front** legs as follows: slip 1 onto the right needle purlwise, insert the right needle through the 2nd stitch from back to front and slip it onto the right needle, thus moving the back leg to the front, return both stitches onto the left needle, now knit 2 together through the **front** legs, yarn over forward (i.e., from yourself)* repeat from * to * until the end of the row before the edge stitch—the last 5 stitches—knit 1 through the **back** leg as follows: insert the right needle through the front leg from front to back and slip it onto the right needle, thus moving the front leg to the back, return this stitch onto the left needle, now knit it through the **back** leg, knit the next 4.

Row 2: Purl 4, purl 1 through the **front** leg as follows: insert the right needle through the front leg from front to back and slip it onto the right needle, thus moving the front leg to the back, return this stitch onto the left needle, now purl it through the **front** leg, *yarn over backward (i.e., to yourself), purl 1, purl 2 together, purl 9* repeat from * to * until the end of the row.

Row 3: *Knit 8, knit 2 together through the **front** legs as described on row 1, knit 2, yarn over forward (i.e., from yourself)* repeat from * to * until the end of the row before the edge stitch, knit the last 5 before the edge stitch as follows: knit 1 through the **back** leg as described in row 1, knit 4.

Row 4: Purl 5 as follows: purl 4, purl 1 through the **front** leg as described in row 2, *yarn over **backward** (i.e., to yourself), purl 3, purl 2 together, purl 7* repeat from * to * until the end of the row.

Row 5: *Knit 6, knit 2 together through the **front** legs as described in row 1, knit 4, yarn over forward (i.e., from yourself)* repeat from * to * until the end of the row before the edge stitch, knit the last 5 before the edge stitch as follows: knit 1 through the **back** leg as described in row 1, knit 4.

Row 6: Purl 5 as follows: purl 4, purl 1 through the **front** leg as described in row 2, *yarn over **backward** (i.e., to yourself), purl 5, purl 2 together, purl 5* repeat from * to * until the end of the row.

Row 7: *Knit 4, knit 2 together through the **front** legs as described in row 1, knit 6, yarn over forward (i.e., from yourself)* repeat from * to * until the end of the row before the edge stitch, knit the last 5 before the edge stitch as follows: knit 1 through the **back** leg as described in row 1, knit 4.

Row 8: Purl 5 as follows: purl 4, purl 1 through the **front** leg as described in row 2, *yarn over **backward** (i.e., to yourself), purl 7, purl 2 together, purl 3* repeat from * to * until the end of the row.

Row 9: *Knit 2, knit 2 together as described in row 1, knit 8, yarn over forward (i.e., from yourself)* repeat from * to * until the end of the row before the edge stitch, knit the last 5 as follows: knit 1 through the **back** leg as described in row 1, knit 4.

Row 10: Purl 5 as follows: purl 4, purl 1 through the **front** leg as described in row 2, *yarn over **backward** (i.e., to yourself), purl 9, purl 2 together, purl 1* repeat from * to * until the end of the row.

Row 11: *Knit 2 together as described in row 1, knit 10, yarn over forward (i.e., from yourself)* repeat from * to * until the end of the row before the edge stitch, knit the last 5 as follows: knit 1 through the **back** leg as described in row 1, knit 4.

Row 12: Purl all the stitches.

Row 13: Knit all the stitches.

Row 14: *Purl 10, purl the next 2 together as follows, to receive the stitch on the front side with a slant to the left: insert the right needle through the back legs of both stitches simultaneously from left to right and slip these 2 stitches onto the right needle, thus moving the back legs to the front, return both stitches onto the left needle, now purl 2 together through the front legs, yarn over **backward** (i.e., to yourself)* repeat from * to * until the end of the row before the edge stitch—the last 5—purl 1 through the front leg as follows: insert the right needle through the back leg from back to front and slip it onto the right needle, thus moving the back leg to the front, return this stitch onto the left needle, now purl 1 through the **front** leg, then purl 4.

Row 15: Knit 5 as follows: knit 4 through the back legs, knit 1 through the **back** leg as follows: insert the right needle through the back leg from back to front and slip it onto the right needle, thus moving the back leg to the front, return this stitch onto the left needle, now knit it through the **back** leg too, *yarn over forward (i.e., from yourself), knit 1, knit 2 together through the **back** legs as follows: slip the 1st stitch onto the right needle, turn the 2nd one on the left needle clockwise twice as follows: insert the right needle through the back leg from back to front and slip it onto the right needle, thus moving the back leg to the front, return this stitch onto the left needle, now the back leg becomes the front one, then insert the right needle through the back leg 1 more time and slip it onto the right needle, thus moving the back leg to the front 1 more time, return this stitch onto the left needle, then return the 1st stitch from the right needle to the left one, now knit 2 together through the **back** legs, then knit 9* repeat from * to * until the end of the row.

Row 16: *Purl 8, purl the next 2 together as described in row 14, to receive the stitch on the front side with a slant to the left, purl 2, yarn over **backward** (i.e., to yourself)* repeat from * to * until the end of the row before the edge stitch—the last 5—purl 1 through the **front** leg as described in row 14, then purl 4.

Row 17: Knit 5 as follows: knit 4 through the **back** legs, knit the next 1 through the **back** leg as described in row 15, *yarn over forward (i.e., from yourself), knit 3, knit 2 together as described in row 15, then knit 7* repeat from * to * until the end of the row.

Row 18: *Purl 6, purl the next 2 together as described in row 14, to receive the stitch on the front side with a slant to the left, purl 4, yarn over **backward** (i.e., to yourself) * repeat from * to * until the end of the row before the edge stitch—the last 5—purl 1 through the **front** leg as described in row 14, then purl 4.

Row 19: Knit 5 as follows: knit 4, knit the next 1 through the **back** leg as described in row 15, *yarn over forward (i.e., from yourself), knit 5, knit 2 together as described in row 15, knit 5* repeat from * to * until the end of the row.

Row 20: *Purl 4, purl the next 2 together as described in row 14, to receive the stitch on the front side with a slant to the left, purl 6, yarn over **backward** (i.e., to yourself) * repeat from * to * until the end of the row before the edge stitch—the last 5—purl 1 through the front leg as described in row 14, then purl 4.

Row 21: Knit 5 as follows: knit 4, knit the next 1 through the **back** leg as described in row 15, *yarn over forward (i.e., from yourself), knit 7, knit 2 together as described in row 15, knit 3* repeat from * to * until the end of the row.

Row 22: *Purl 2, purl the next 2 together as described in row 14, to receive the stitch on the front side with a slant to the left, purl 8, yarn over **backward** (i.e., to yourself) * repeat from * to * until the end of the row before the edge stitch—the last 5—purl 1 through the front leg as described in row 14, then purl 4.

Row 23: Knit 5 as follows: knit 4, knit the next 1 through the **back** leg as described in row 15, *yarn over forward (i.e., from yourself), knit 9, knit 2 together as described in row 15, knit 1* repeat from * to * until the end of the row.

Row 24: *Purl 2 together as described in row 14, to receive the stitch on the front side with a slant to the left, purl 10, yarn over **backward** (i.e., to yourself)* repeat from * to * until the end of the row before the edge stitch—the last 5—purl 1 through the **front** leg as described in row 14, then purl 4.

Row 25: Knit all the stitches.

Row 26: Purl all the stitches.

Repeat rows: 1-26.

Bind off after the last row 24 as follows: Slip the edge stitch onto the right needle, knit the next 1, then insert the left needle through the slipped edge stitch, from left to right, and pass it over the knitted stitch, *now there is 1 stitch on the right needle, knit the next 1 (now there are 2 stitches on the right needle), insert the left needle through the 1st stitch on the right needle from left to right and pass it over the 2nd one* repeat from * to * until the end of the row.

Pattern 35

Cast on a multiple of 9, plus 2 edge stitches. Nine-stitch repeat. Repeat rows: 1-8. **The edge stitches are not included in the description below and must be added. Slip the first edge stitch, purl the last one.**

Knit through the back leg, purl as follows: with the working yarn in front of the stitch, insert the right needle through the stitch from back to front, move the working yarn under the right needle and pull it with the needle through the stitch. The purl stitch that works this way sets up the knit stitch for knitting through the back leg. **Needles: 2.5 mm.**

Description:

Row 1: *Knit 4, yarn over forward (i.e., from yourself), knit 2 together through the **back** legs as follows: slip the 1st stitch onto the right needle, turn the next 1 on the left needle clockwise twice as follows: insert the right needle through the back leg from back to front and slip it onto the right needle, thus moving the back leg to the front, return this stitch onto the left needle, now the back leg becomes the front one, then insert the right needle through the back leg 1 more time and slip the stitch onto the right needle, thus moving the back leg to the front 1 more time, return this stitch onto the left needle, then return the 1st slipped stitch from the right needle to the left one, now knit 2 together through the **back** legs, knit 3* repeat from * to * until the end of the row.

Row 2: Purl all the stitches.

Row 3: *Knit 2, knit 2 together through the **front** legs as follows: turn the first 1 on the left needle clockwise twice as follows: insert the right needle through the back leg from back to front and slip it onto the right needle, thus moving the back leg to the front, return this stitch onto the left needle, now the back leg becomes the front one, then insert the right needle through the back leg 1 more time and slip it onto the right needle, thus moving the back leg to the front 1 more time, leave this stitch on the right needle, insert the right needle through the back leg of the 2nd stitch from back to front and slip it onto the right needle, thus moving the back leg to the front, return both stitches onto the left needle, now knit 2 together through the **front** legs, yarn over forward (i.e., from yourself), knit 1, yarn over forward (i.e., from yourself), knit 2 together through the **back** legs as described in row 1, knit 2* repeat from * to * until the end of the row.

Row 4: Purl all the stitches.

Row 5: *Knit 1, knit 2 together through the **front** legs as described in row 3, yarn over forward (i.e., from yourself), knit 3, yarn over forward (i.e., from yourself), knit 2 together through the **back** legs as described in row 1, knit 1* repeat from * to * until the end of the row.

Row 6: Purl all the stitches.

Row 7: *Knit 2 together through the **front** legs as described in row 3, yarn over forward (i.e., from yourself), knit 5, yarn over forward (i.e., from yourself), knit 2 together through the **back** legs as described in row 1* repeat from * to * until the end of the row.

Row 8: Purl all the stitches.

Repeat rows: 1-8.

Bind off after the last row 8 as follows: Slip the edge stitch onto the right needle, knit the next 1, then insert the left needle through the slipped edge stitch, from left to right, and pass it over the knitted stitch, *now there is 1 stitch on the right needle, knit the next 1 (now there are 2 stitches on the right needle), insert the left needle through the 1st stitch on the right needle, from left to right, and pass it over the 2nd one* repeat from * to * until the end of the row.

Pattern 36

Cast on a multiple of 9, plus 2 edge stitches. Nine-stitch repeat. Repeat rows: 1-8. **The edge stitches are not included in the description below and must be added. Slip the first edge stitch, purl the last one.**

Knit through the back leg, purl as follows: with the working yarn in front of the stitch, insert the right needle through the stitch from back to front, move the working yarn under the right needle and pull it with the needle through the stitch. The purl stitch that works this way sets up the knit stitch for knitting through the back leg. **Needles: 2.5 mm.**

Description:

Row 1: *Knit 3, knit 2 together through the **front** legs as follows: turn the first 1 on the left needle clockwise twice as follows: insert the right needle through the back leg from back to front and slip it onto the right needle, thus moving the back leg to the front, return this stitch onto the left needle, now the back leg becomes the front one, then insert the right needle through the back leg 1 more time and slip the stitch onto the right needle, thus moving the back leg to the front 1 more time, leave this stitch on the right needle, insert the right needle through the back leg of the next stitch from back to front and slip it onto the right needle, thus moving the back leg to the front, return both stitches onto the left needle, now knit 2 together through the **front** legs, yarn over forward (i.e., from yourself), knit 1, yarn over forward (i.e., from yourself), knit 2 together through the **back** legs as follows: slip the 1st stitch onto the right needle, turn the next 1 on the left needle clockwise twice as follows: insert the right needle through the back leg from back to front and slip it onto the right needle, thus moving the back leg to the front, return this stitch onto the left needle, now the back leg becomes the front one, then insert the right needle through the back leg 1 more time and slip it onto the right needle, thus moving the back leg to the front 1 more time, return this stitch onto the left needle, then return the 1st stitch onto the left needle, now knit 2 together through the **back** legs, knit 1* repeat from * to * until the end of the row.

Row 2: Purl all the stitches.

Row 3: *Knit 2, knit 2 together through the **front** legs as described in row 1, yarn over forward (i.e., from yourself), knit 3, yarn over forward (i.e., from yourself), knit 2 together through the **back** legs as described in row 1* repeat from * to * until the end of the row.

Row 4: Purl all the stitches.

Row 5: *Knit 1, knit 2 together through the **front** legs as described in row 1, yarn over forward (i.e., from yourself), knit 1, yarn over forward (i.e., from yourself), knit 2 together through the **back** legs as described in row 1, knit 3* repeat from * to * until the end of the row.

Row 6: Purl all the stitches.

Row 7: *Knit 2 together through the **front** legs as described in row 1, yarn over forward (i.e., from yourself), knit 3, yarn over forward (i.e., from yourself), knit 2 together through the **back** legs as described in row 1, knit 2* repeat from * to * until the end of the row.

Row 8: Purl all the stitches.

Repeat rows: 1-8.

Bind off after the last row 8 as follows: Slip the edge stitch onto the right needle, knit the next 1, then insert the left needle through the slipped edge stitch, from left to right, and pass it over the knitted stitch, *now there is 1 stitch on the right needle, knit the next 1 (now there are 2 stitches on the right needle), insert the left needle through the 1st stitch on the right needle, from left to right, and pass it over the 2nd one* repeat from * to * until the end of the row.

Pattern 37

Cast on a multiple of 18, plus 2 edge stitches. Eighteen-stitch repeat. Repeat rows: 1-12. **The edge stitches are not included in the description below and must be added. Slip the first edge stitch, purl the last one.**

Knit through the back leg, purl as follows: with the working yarn in front of the stitch, insert the right needle through the stitch from back to front, move the working yarn under the right needle and pull it with the needle through the stitch. The purl stitch that works this way sets up the knit stitch for knitting through the back leg. **Needles: 2.5 mm.**

Description:

Row 1: *Knit 2, knit 2 together through the **front** legs as follows: turn the 1st one on the left needle clockwise twice as follows: insert the right needle through the back leg from back to front and slip it onto the right needle, thus moving the back leg to the front, return this stitch onto the left needle, now the back leg becomes the front one, then insert the right needle through the back leg 1 more time and it onto the right needle, thus moving the back leg to the front 1 more time, leave this stitch on the right needle, insert the right needle through the back leg of the 2nd stitch from back to front and slip it onto the right needle, thus moving the back leg to the front, return both stitches onto the left needle, now knit 2 together through the **front** legs, yarn over forward (i.e., from yourself), knit 3, yarn over forward (i.e., from yourself), knit 2 together through the **back** legs as follows: slip the 1st stitch onto the right needle, turn the next 1 on the left needle clockwise twice as follows: insert the right needle through the back leg from back to front and slip it onto the right needle, thus moving the back leg to the front, return this stitch onto the left needle, now the back leg becomes the front one, then insert the right needle through the back leg 1 more time and it onto the right needle, thus moving the back leg to the front 1 more time, return this stitch onto the left needle, then return the 1st stitch onto the left one, now knit 2 together through the **back** legs, knit 2 together through the **front** legs as described in this row above, yarn over forward (i.e., from yourself), knit 3, yarn over forward (i.e., from yourself), knit 2 together through the **back** legs as described in this row above, knit 2* repeat from * to * until the end of the row.

Row 2: Purl all the stitches.

Row 3: *Knit 1, knit 2 together through the **front** legs as described in row 1, yarn over forward (i.e., from yourself), knit 4, yarn over forward (i.e., from yourself), knit 2 together through the **back** legs as described in row 1, knit 2 together through the **front** legs as described in row 1, yarn over forward (i.e., from yourself), knit 4, yarn over forward (i.e., from yourself), knit 2 together through the **back** legs as described in row 1, knit 1* repeat from * to * until the end of the row.

Row 4: Purl all the stitches.

Row 5: *Knit 2 together through the **front** legs as described in row 1, yarn over forward (i.e., from yourself), knit 5, yarn over forward (i.e., from yourself), knit 2 together through the **back** legs as described in row 1, knit 2 together through the **front** legs as described in row 1, yarn over forward (i.e., from yourself), knit 5, yarn over forward (i.e., from yourself), knit 2 together through the **back** legs as described in row 1* repeat from * to * until the end of the row.

Row 6: Purl all the stitches.

Row 7: *Knit 2 together through the **front** legs as described in row 1, yarn over forward (i.e., from yourself), knit 3, knit 2 together through the **front** legs as described in row 1, yarn over forward (i.e., from yourself), knit 4, yarn over forward (i.e., from yourself), knit 2 together through the **back** legs as described in row 1, knit 3, yarn over forward (i.e., from yourself), knit 2 together through the **back** legs as described in row 1* repeat from * to * until the end of the row.

Row 8: Purl all the stitches.

Row 9: *Knit 2 together through the **front** legs as described in row 1, yarn over forward (i.e., from yourself), knit 2, knit 2 together through the **front** legs as described in row 1, yarn over forward (i.e., from yourself), knit 6, yarn over forward (i.e., from yourself), knit 2 together through the **back** legs as described in row 1, knit 2, yarn over forward (i.e., from yourself), knit 2 together
through the **back** legs as described in row 1* repeat from * to * until the end of the row.

Row 10: Purl all the stitches.

Row 11: *Knit 3, knit 2 together through the **front** legs as described in row 1, yarn over forward (i.e., from yourself), knit 8, yarn over forward (i.e., from yourself), knit 2 together through the **back** legs as described in row 1, knit 3* repeat from * to * until the end of the row.

Row 12: Purl all the stitches.

Repeat rows: 1-12.

Bind off after the last row 12 as follows: Slip the edge stitch onto the right needle, knit the next 1, then insert the left needle through the slipped edge stitch, from left to right, and pass it over the knitted stitch, *now there is 1 stitch on the right needle, knit the next 1 (now there are 2 stitches on the right needle), insert the left needle through the 1st stitch on the right needle, from left to right, and pass it over the 2nd one* repeat from * to * until the end of the row.

Pattern 38

Cast on a multiple of 10, plus 4, and 2 edge stitches. Ten-stitch repeat. Repeat rows: 1-10. **The edge stitches are not included in the description below and must be added. Slip the first edge stitch, purl the last one.**

Knit through the back leg, purl as follows: with the working yarn in front of the stitch, insert the right needle through the stitch from back to front, move the working yarn under the right needle and pull it with the needle through the stitch. The purl stitch that works this way sets up the knit stitch for knitting through the back leg. **Needles: 3 mm.**

Description:

Row 1: Knit 4, *knit 2 together through the **front** legs as follows: turn the 1st one on the left needle clockwise twice as follows: insert the right needle through the back leg from back to front and slip it onto the right needle, thus moving the back leg to the front, return this stitch onto the left needle, now the back leg becomes the front one, then insert the right needle through the back leg 1 more time and slip it onto the right needle, thus moving the back leg to the front 1 more time, leave this stitch on the right needle, insert the right needle through the back leg of the 2nd stitch from back to front and slip it onto the right needle, thus moving the back leg to the front, return both stitches onto the left needle, now knit 2 together through the **front** legs, knit 2, yarn over forward (i.e., from yourself), knit 6* repeat from * to * until the end of the row.

Row 2: Purl 1, *purl 6, yarn over forward (i.e., from yourself), purl 2, purl 2 together* repeat from * to * until the end of the row before the edge stitch, purl 3.

Row 3: Knit 2, *knit 2 together through the **front** legs as described in row 1, knit 2, yarn over forward (i.e., from yourself), knit 6* repeat from * to * until the end of the row before the edge stitch, knit 2.

Row 4: Yarn over forward (i.e., from yourself), purl 1, purl 2 together, *purl 6, yarn over forward (i.e., from yourself), purl 2, purl 2 together* repeat from * to * until the end of the row before the edge stitch, purl 1.

Row 5: *Knit 2 together through the **front** legs as described in row 1, knit 2, yarn over forward (i.e., from yourself), knit 6* repeat from * to * until the end of the row before the edge stitch, knit 2 together through the **front** legs as described in row 1, knit 2, yarn over forward (i.e., from yourself).

Row 6: Purl 4, *purl the next 2 together as follows, in order to receive the stitch on front side with a slant to the left: slip the 1st stitch onto the right needle, insert the right needle through the 2nd stitch from front to back and slip it onto the right needle, thus moving the front leg to the back, return both stitches onto the left needle, insert the right needle through the back legs of these 2 stitches simultaneously from left to right and slip both stitches onto the right needle, thus moving the back legs to the front, return both stitches onto the left needle, now purl 2 together through the **front** legs, purl 2, yarn over forward (i.e., from yourself), purl 6* repeat from * to * until the end of the row.

Row 7: Knit 1, *knit 6, yarn over forward (i.e., from yourself), knit 2, knit 2 together through the **back** legs as follows: slip the 1st stitch onto the right needle, turn the 2nd one on left needle clockwise twice as follows: insert the right needle through the back leg from back to front and slip it onto the right needle, thus moving the back leg to the front, return this stitch onto the left needle, now the back leg becomes the front one, then insert the right needle through the back leg 1 more time and it onto the right needle, thus moving the back leg to the front 1 more time, return this stitch onto the left needle, then return the 1st stitch from the right needle to the left one, now knit 2 together through the **back** legs* repeat from * to * until the end of the row before the edge stitch, knit 3.

Row 8: Purl 2, *purl the next 2 together as described in row 6, to receive the stitch on the right side with a slant to the left, purl 2, yarn over forward (i.e., from yourself), purl 6* repeat from * to * until the end of the row before the edge stitch, purl 2.

Row 9: Yarn over forward (i.e., to yourself), knit 1, knit 2 together through the **back** legs as described in row 7, *knit 6, yarn over forward (i.e., from yourself), knit 2, knit 2 together through the **back** legs as described in row 7* repeat from * to * until the end of the row before the edge stitch, knit 1.

Row 10: *Purl 2 together as described in row 6, to receive the stitch on the front side with a slant to the left, purl 2, yarn over forward (i.e., from yourself), purl 6* repeat from * to * until the end of the row before the edge stitch, purl the next 2 together as described in row 6, to receive the stitch on the front side with a slant to the left, purl 2, yarn over forward (i.e., from yourself).

Repeat rows: 1-10.

Bind off after the last row 10 as follows: Slip the edge stitch onto the right needle, knit the next 1, then insert the left needle through the slipped edge stitch, from left to right, and pass it over the knitted stitch, *now there is 1 stitch on the right needle, knit the next 1 (now there are 2 stitches on the right needle), insert the left needle through the 1st stitch on the right needle, from left to right, and pass it over the 2nd one* repeat from * to * until the end of the row.

Pattern 39

Cast on 19 for the braid; the number of adjacent stitches is optional. Repeat rows: 1-6.

Knit through the back leg, purl as follows: with the working yarn in front of the stitch, insert the right needle through the stitch from back to front, move the working yarn under the right needle and pull it with the needle through the stitch. The purl stitch that works this way sets up the knit stitch for knitting through the back leg. **Needles: 2.5 mm.**

Description:

Row 1: Knit 5, knit 2 together through the **front** legs as follows: turn the 1st one on the left needle clockwise twice as follows: insert the right needle through the back leg from back to front and slip it onto the right needle, thus moving the back leg to the front, return this stitch onto the left needle, now the back leg becomes the front one, then insert the right needle through the back leg 1 more time and slip it onto the right needle, thus moving the back leg to the front 1 more time, leave this stitch on the right needle, insert the right needle through the back leg of the 2nd stitch from back to front and slip it onto the right needle, thus moving the back leg to the front, return both stitches onto the left needle, now knit 2 together through the **front** legs, knit 2, yarn over forward (i.e., from yourself), purl 1, yarn over forward (i.e., from yourself), knit 2, knit 2 together through the **back** legs as follows: slip the 1st stitch onto the right needle, turn the next 1 on the left needle clockwise twice as follows: insert the right needle through the back leg from back to front and slip it onto the right needle, thus moving the back leg to the front, return this stitch onto the left needle, now the back leg becomes the front one, then insert the right needle through the back leg 1 more time and slip it onto the right needle, thus moving the back leg to the front 1 more time, return this stitch onto the left needle, then return the 1st stitch from the right needle to the left one, now knit 2 together through the **back** legs, knit 5.

Row 2: Purl 4, purl the next 2 together in order to receive the stitch on the front side with a slant to the left: insert the right needle through the back legs of these 2 stitches simultaneously from left to right and slip both stitches onto the right needle, thus moving the back legs to the front, return both stitches onto the left needle, now purl 2 together through the front legs, purl 2, yarn over **backward** (i.e., to yourself), purl 1, knit 1, purl 1, yarn over **backward** (i.e., to yourself), purl 2, purl 2 together, purl 4.

Row 3: Knit 3, knit 2 together through the **front** legs as described in row 1, knit 2, yarn over forward (i.e., from yourself), knit 2, purl 1, knit 2, yarn over forward (i.e., from yourself), knit 2, knit 2 together through the **back** legs as described in row 1, knit 3.

Row 4: Purl 2, purl the next 2 together with a slant to the left as described in row 2, to receive the stitch on the front side with a slant to the left, purl 2, yarn over **backward** (i.e., to yourself), purl 3, knit 1, purl 3, yarn over **backward** (i.e., to yourself), purl 2, purl 2 together, purl 2.

Row 5: Knit 1, knit 2 together through the **front** legs as described in row 1, knit 2, yarn over forward (i.e., from yourself), knit 4, purl 1, knit 4, yarn over forward (i.e., from yourself), knit 2, knit 2 together through the **back** legs as described in row 1, knit 1.

Row 6: Purl 2 together with a slant to the left as described in row 2, purl 2, yarn over **backward** (i.e., to yourself), purl 5, knit 1, purl 5, yarn over **backward** (i.e., to yourself), purl 2, purl 2 together.

Repeat rows: 1-6.

Bind off as follows: Slip the edge stitch onto the right needle, knit the next 1, then insert the left needle through the slipped edge stitch, from left to right, and pass it over the knitted stitch, *now there is 1 stitch on the right needle, knit the next 1 (now there are 2 stitches on the right needle), insert the left needle through the 1st stitch on the right needle, from left to right, and pass it over the 2nd one* repeat from * to * until the end of the row.

Pattern 40

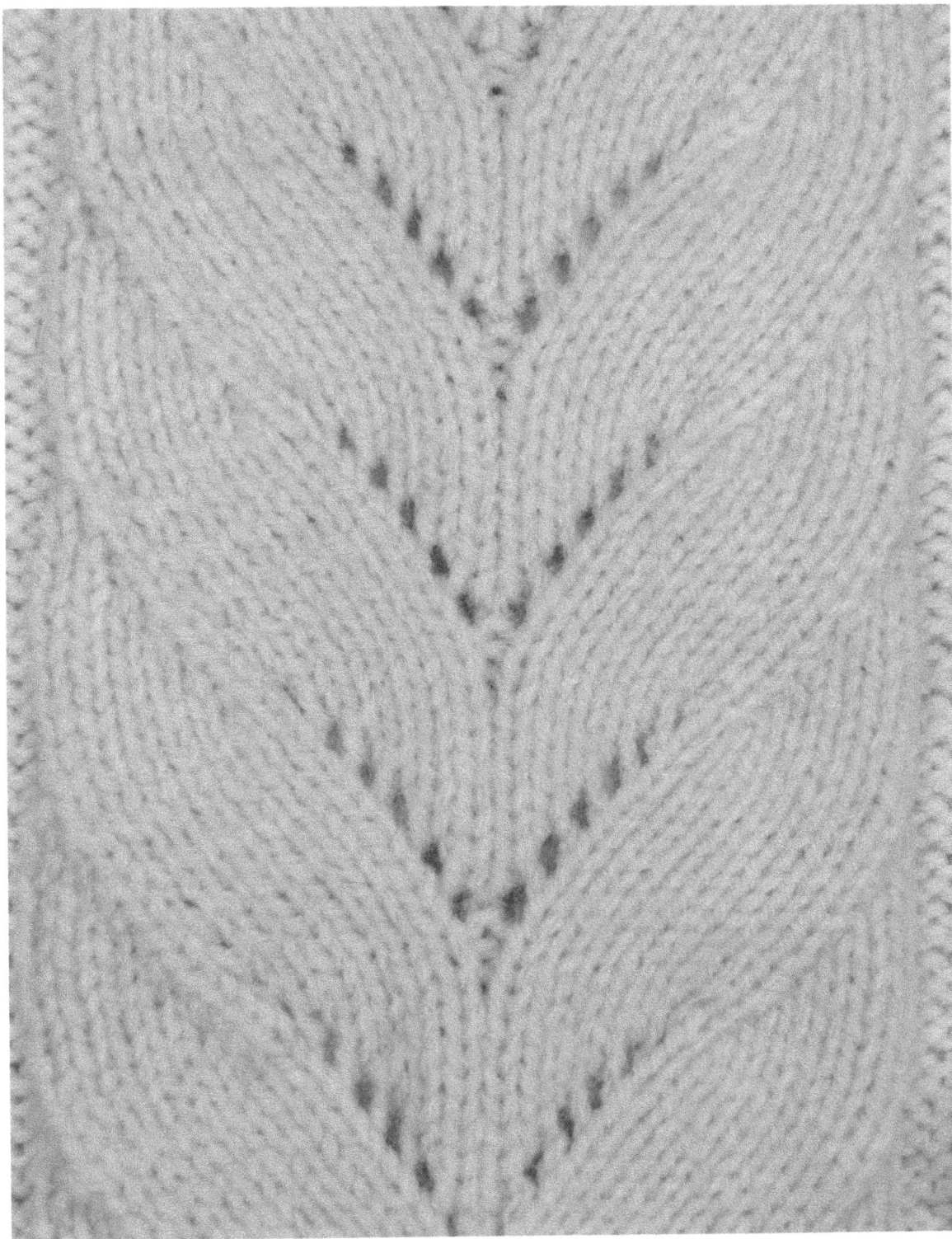

Cast on 27 for the braid; the number of adjacent stitches is optional. Repeat rows: 1-12.

Repeat rows: 1-6.

Bind off as follows: Slip the edge stitch onto the right needle, knit the next 1, then insert the left needle through the slipped edge stitch, from left to right, and pass it over the knitted stitch, *now there is 1 stitch on the right needle, knit the next 1 (now there are 2 stitches on the right needle), insert the left needle through the 1st stitch on the right needle, from left to right, and pass it over the 2nd one* repeat from * to * until the end of the row.

Pattern 40

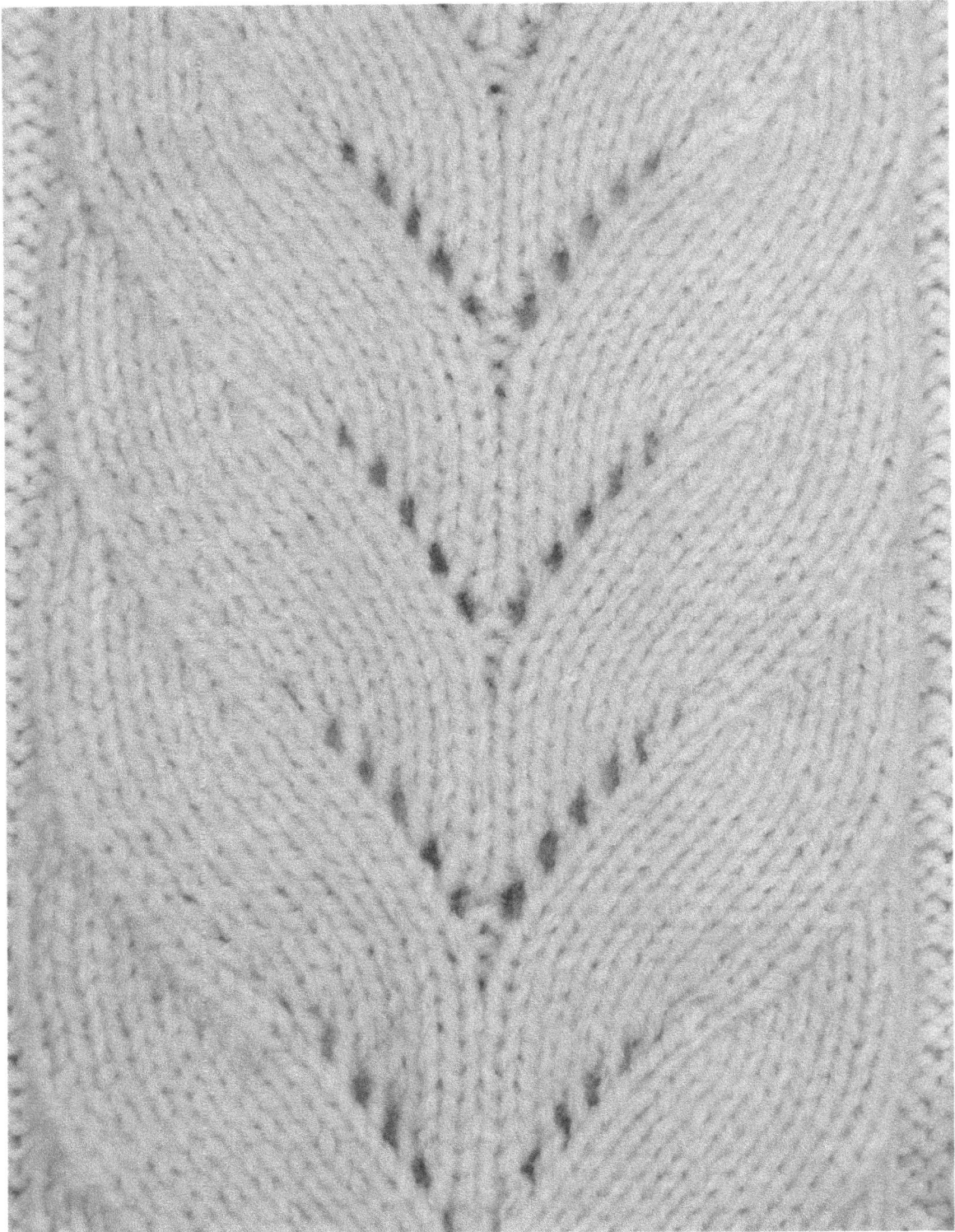

Cast on 27 for the braid; the number of adjacent stitches is optional. Repeat rows: 1-12.

Knit through the back leg, purl as follows: with the working yarn in front of the stitch, insert the right needle through the stitch from back to front, move the working yarn under the right needle and pull it with the needle through the stitch. The purl stitch that works this way sets up the knit stitch for knitting through the back leg. **Needles: 2.5 mm.**

Description:

Row 1: Knit 5, knit 2 together through the **front** legs as follows: turn the 1st one on the left needle clockwise twice as follows: insert the right needle through the back leg from back to front and slip it onto the right needle, thus moving the back leg to the front, return this stitch onto the left needle, now the back leg becomes the front one, then insert the right needle through the back leg 1 more time and slip the stitch onto the right needle, thus moving the back leg to the front 1 more time, leave this stitch on the right needle, insert the right needle through the back leg of the 2nd stitch from back to front and slip it onto the right needle, thus moving the back leg to the front, return both stitches onto the left needle, now knit 2 together through the **front** legs, knit 6, yarn over forward (i.e., from yourself), purl 1, yarn over forward (i.e., from yourself), knit 6, knit 2 together through the **back** legs as follows: slip the 1st stitch onto the right needle, turn the next 1 on the left needle clockwise twice as follows: insert the right needle through the back leg from back to front and slip it onto the right needle, thus moving the back leg to the front, return this stitch onto the left needle, now the back leg becomes the front one, then insert the right needle through the back leg 1 more time and slip the stitch onto the right needle, thus moving the back leg to the front 1 more time, return this stitch onto the left needle, then return the 1st stitch onto the left needle, now knit 2 together through the **back** legs, knit 5.

Row 2: Purl 13, knit 1, purl 13.

Row 3: Knit 4, knit 2 together through the **front** legs as described in row 1, knit 6, yarn over forward (i.e., from yourself), knit 1, purl 1, knit 1, yarn over forward (i.e., from yourself), knit 6, knit 2 together through the **back** legs as described in row 1, knit 4.

Row 4: Purl 13, knit 1, purl 13.

Row 5: Knit 3, knit 2 together through the **front** legs as described in row 1, knit 6, yarn over forward (i.e., from yourself), knit 2, purl 1, knit 2, yarn over forward (i.e., from yourself), knit 6, knit 2 together through the **back** legs as described in row 1, knit 3.

Row 6: Purl 13, knit 1, purl 13.

Row 7: Knit 2, knit 2 together through the **front** legs as described in row 1, knit 6, yarn over forward (i.e., from yourself), knit 3, purl 1, knit 3, yarn over forward (i.e., from yourself), knit 6, knit 2 together through the **back** legs as described in row 1, knit 2.

Row 8: Purl 13, knit 1, purl 13.

Row 9: Knit 1, knit 2 together through the **front** legs as described in row 1, knit 6, yarn over forward (i.e., from yourself), knit 4, purl 1, knit 4, yarn over forward (i.e., from yourself), knit 6, knit 2 together through the **back** legs as described in row 1, knit 1.

Row 10: Purl 13, knit 1, purl 13.

Row 11: Knit 2 together through the **front** legs as described in row 1, knit 6, yarn over forward (i.e., from yourself), knit 5, purl 1, knit 5, yarn over forward (i.e., from yourself), knit 6, knit 2 together through the **back** legs as described in row 1.

Row 12: Purl 13, knit 1, purl 13.

Repeat rows: 1-12.

Bind off after the last row 12 as follows: Slip the edge stitch onto the right needle, knit the next 1, then insert the left needle through the slipped edge stitch, from left to right, and pass it over the knitted stitch, *now there is 1 stitch on the right needle, knit the next 1 (now there are 2 stitches on the right needle), insert the left needle through the 1st stitch on the right needle, from left to right, and pass it over the 2nd one* repeat from * to * until the end of the row.

Pattern 41

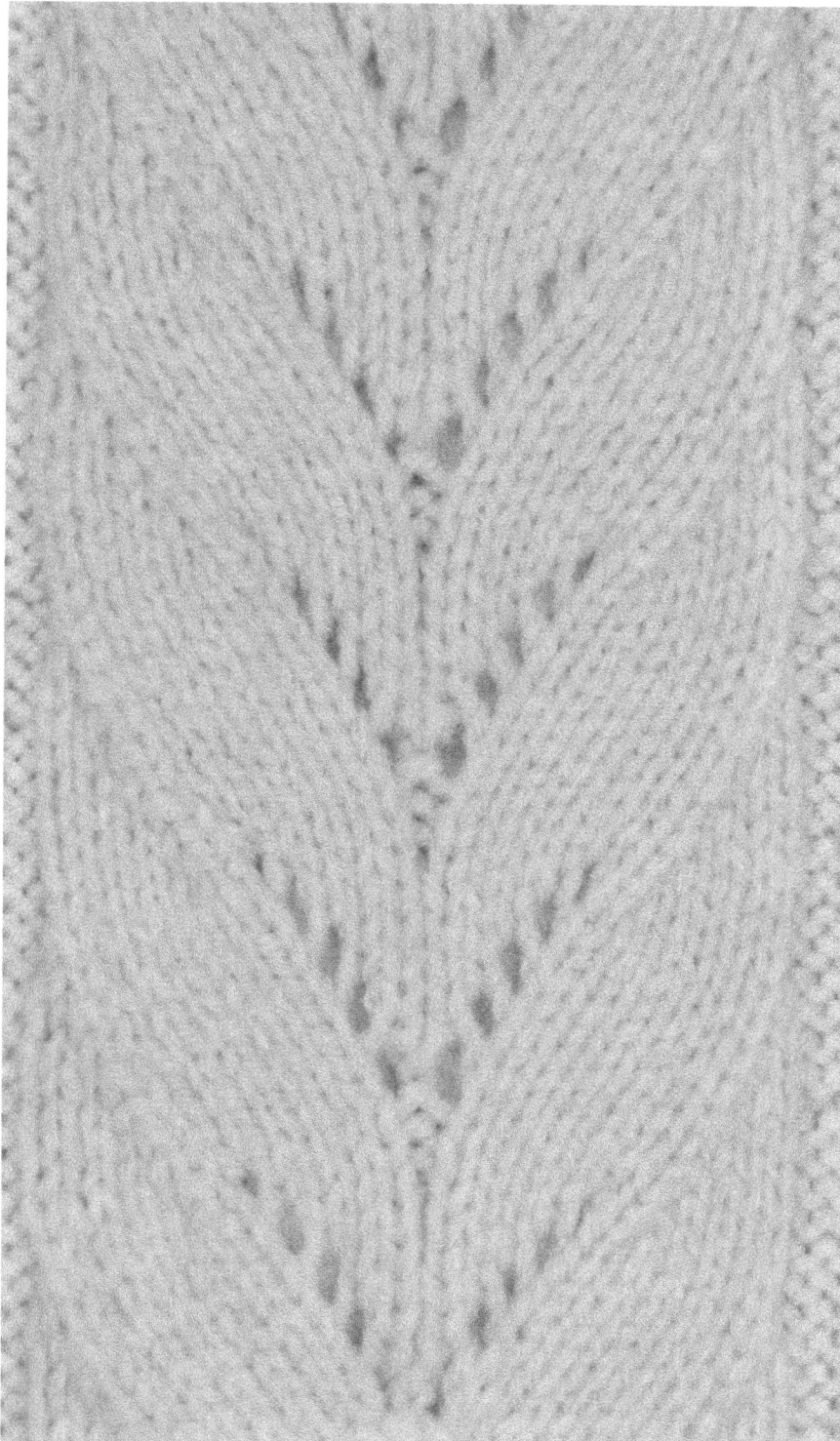

Cast on 23 for the braid; the number of adjacent stitches is optional. Repeat rows: 1-10.

Knit through the back leg, purl as follows: with the working yarn in front of the stitch, insert the right needle through the stitch from back to front, move the working yarn under the right needle and pull it with the needle through the stitch. The purl stitch that works this way sets up the knit stitch for knitting through the back leg. **Needles: 2.5 mm.**

Description:

Row 1: Knit 4, knit 2 together through the **front** legs as follows: turn the 1st one on the left needle clockwise twice as follows: insert the right needle through the back leg from back to front and slip it onto the right needle, thus moving the back leg to the front, return this stitch onto the left needle, now the back leg becomes the front one, then insert the right needle through the back leg 1 more time and slip the stitch onto the right needle, thus moving the back leg to the front 1 more time, leave this stitch on the right needle, insert the right needle through the back leg of the 2nd stitch from back to front and slip it onto the right needle, thus moving the back leg to the front, return both stitches onto the left needle, now knit 2 together through the **front** legs,knit 5, yarn over forward (i.e., from yourself), purl 1, yarn over forward (i.e., from yourself), knit 5, knit 2 together through the **back** legs as follows: slip the 1st stitch onto the right needle, turn the 2nd one on the left needle clockwise twice as follows: insert the right needle through the back leg from back to front and slip it onto the right needle, thus moving the back leg to the front, return this stitch onto the left needle, now the back leg becomes the front one, then insert the right needle through the back leg 1 more time and slip it onto the right needle, thus moving the back leg to the front 1 more time, return this stitch onto the left needle, then return the 1st slipped stitch from the right needle to the left one, now knit 2 together through the **back** legs, knit 4.

Row 2: Purl 11, knit 1, purl 11.

Row 3: Knit 3, knit 2 together through the **front** legs as described in row 1, knit 5, yarn over forward (i.e., from yourself), knit 1, purl 1, knit 1, yarn over forward (i.e., from yourself), knit 5, knit 2 together through the **back** legs as described in row 1, knit 3.

Row 4: Purl 11, knit 1, purl 11.

Row 5: Knit 2, knit 2 together through the **front** legs as described in row 1, knit 5, yarn over forward (i.e., from yourself), knit 2, purl 1, knit 2, yarn over forward (i.e., from yourself), knit 5, knit 2 together through the **back** legs as described in row 1, knit 2.

Row 6: Purl 11, knit 1, purl 11.

Row 7: Knit 1, knit 2 together through the **front** legs as described in row 1, knit 5, yarn over forward (i.e., from yourself), knit 3, purl 1, knit 3, yarn over forward (i.e., from yourself), knit 5, knit 2 together through the **back** legs as described in row 1, knit 1.

Row 8: Purl 11, knit 1, purl 11.

Row 9: Knit 2 together through the **front** legs as described in row 1, knit 5, yarn over forward (i.e., from yourself), knit 4, purl 1, knit 4, yarn over forward (i.e., from yourself), knit 5, knit 2 together through the **back** legs as described in row 1.

Row 10: Purl 11, knit 1, purl 11.

Repeat rows: 1-10.

Bind off as follows: Slip the edge stitch onto the right needle, knit the next 1, then insert the left needle through the slipped edge stitch, from left to right, and pass it over the knitted stitch, *now there is 1 stitch on the right needle, knit the next 1 (now there are 2 stitches on the right needle), insert the left needle through the 1st stitch on the right needle, from left to right, and pass it over the 2nd one* repeat from * to * until the end of the row.

Pattern 42

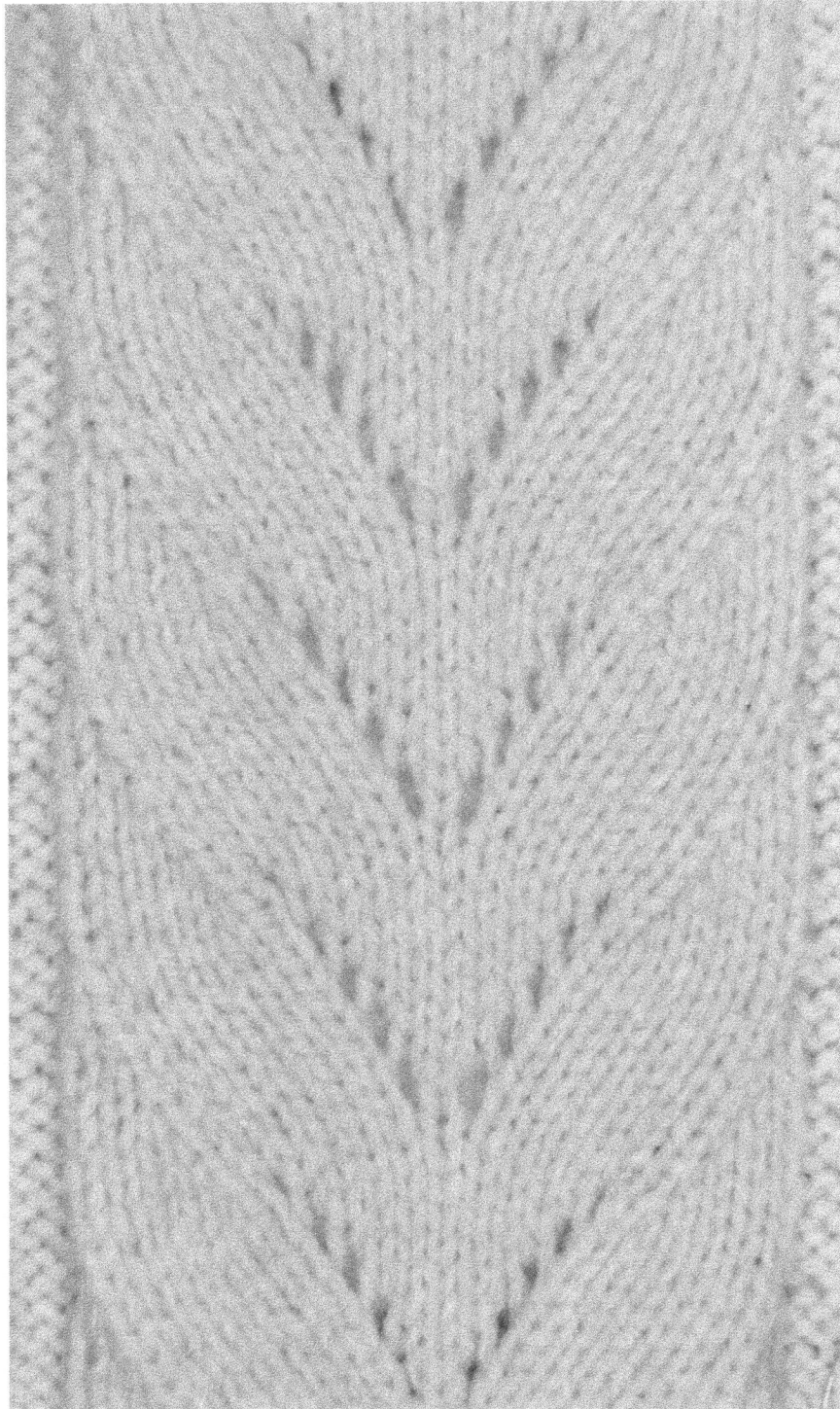

Cast on 23 for the braid; the number of adjacent stitches is optional. Repeat rows: 1-10.

Knit through the back leg, purl as follows: with the working yarn in front of the stitch, insert the right needle through the stitch from back to front, move the working yarn under the right needle and pull it with the needle through the stitch. The purl stitch that works this way sets up the knit stitch for knitting through the back leg. **Needles: 2.5 mm.**

Description:

Row 1: Knit 4, knit 2 together through the **front** legs as follows: turn the 1st one on the left needle clockwise twice as follows: insert the right needle through the back leg from back to front and slip it onto the right needle, thus moving the back leg to the front, return this stitch onto the left needle, now the back leg becomes the front one, then insert the right needle through the back leg 1 more time and slip it onto the right needle, thus moving the back leg to the front 1 more time, leave this stitch on the right needle, insert the right needle through the back leg of the 2nd stitch from back to front and slip it onto the right needle, thus moving the back leg to the front, return both stitches onto the left needle, now knit 2 together through the **front** legs, knit 5, yarn over forward (i.e., from yourself), knit 1, yarn over forward (i.e., from yourself), knit 5, knit 2 together through the **back** legs as follows: slip the 1st stitch onto the right needle, turn the 2nd one on the left needle clockwise twice as follows: insert the right needle through the back leg from back to front and slip it onto the right needle, thus moving the back leg to the front, return this stitch onto the left needle, now the back leg becomes the front one, then insert the right needle through the back leg 1 more time and slip it onto the right needle, thus moving the back leg to the front 1 more time, return this stitch onto the left needle, then return the 1st stitch from onto the left needle, now knit 2 together through the **back** legs, knit 4.

Row 2: Purl all the stitches.

Row 3: Knit 3, knit 2 together through the **front** legs as described in row 1, knit 5, yarn over forward (i.e., from yourself), knit 3, yarn over forward (i.e., from yourself), knit 5, knit 2 together through the **back** legs as described in row 1, knit 3.

Row 4: Purl all the stitches.

Row 5: Knit 2, knit 2 together through the **front** legs as described in row 1, knit 5, yarn over forward (i.e., from yourself), knit 5, yarn over forward (i.e., from yourself), knit 5, knit 2 together through the **back** legs as described in row 1, knit 2.

Row 6: Purl all the stitches.

Row 7: Knit 1, knit 2 together through the **front** legs as described in row 1, knit 5, yarn over forward (i.e., from yourself), knit 7, yarn over forward (i.e., from yourself), knit 5, knit 2 together through the **back** legs as described in row 1, knit 1.

Row 8: Purl all the stitches.

Row 9: Knit 2 together through the **front** legs as described in row 1, knit 5, yarn over forward (i.e., from yourself), knit 9, yarn over forward (i.e., from yourself), knit 5, knit 2 together through the **back** legs as described in row 1.

Row 10: Purl all the stitches.
Repeat rows: 1-10.

Bind off as follows: Slip the edge stitch onto the right needle, knit the next 1, then insert the left needle through the slipped edge stitch, from left to right, and pass it over the knitted stitch, *now there is 1 stitch on the right needle, knit the next 1 (now there are 2 stitches on the right needle), insert the left needle through the 1st stitch on the right needle, from left to right, and pass it over the 2nd one* repeat from * to * until the end of the row.

Pattern 43

Cast on a multiple of 13, plus 2 edge stitches. Thirteen-stitch repeat. Repeat rows: 1-8. **The edge stitches are not included in the description below and must be added. Slip the first edge stitch, purl the last one.**

Knit through the back leg, purl as follows: with the working yarn in front of the stitch, insert the right needle through the stitch from back to front, move the working yarn under the right needle and pull it with the needle through the stitch. The purl stitch that works this way sets up the knit stitch for knitting through the back leg. **Needles: 2.5 mm.**

Description:

Row 1: *Knit 3, knit 2 together through the **front** legs as follows: turn the 1st stitch on the left needle clockwise twice as follows: insert the right needle through the back leg from back to front and slip it onto the right needle, thus moving the back leg to the front, return this stitch onto the left needle, now the back leg becomes the front one, then insert the right needle through the back leg 1 more time and slip it onto the right needle, thus moving the back leg to the front 1 more time, leave this stitch on the right needle, insert the right needle through the back leg of the 2nd stitch from back to front and slip it onto the right needle, thus moving the back leg to the front, return both stitches onto the left needle, now knit 2 together through the **front** legs,knit 1, yarn over forward (i.e., from yourself), knit 1, yarn over forward (i.e., from yourself), knit 1, knit 2 together through the **back** legs as follows: slip the 1st stitch onto the right needle, turn the 2nd stitch on the left needle clockwise twice as follows: insert the right needle through the back leg from back to front and slip it onto the right needle, thus moving the back leg to the front, return this stitch onto the left needle, now the back leg becomes the front one, then insert the right needle through the back leg 1 more time and slip it onto the right needle, thus moving the back leg to the front 1 more time, return this stitch onto the left needle, then return the 1st stitch from the right needle to the left one, now knit 2 together through the **back** legs, knit 3* repeat from * to * until the end of the row.

Row 2: Purl all the stitches.

Row 3: *Knit 2, knit 2 together through the **front** legs as described in row 1, knit 1, yarn over forward (i.e., from yourself), knit 3, yarn over forward (i.e., from yourself), knit 1, knit 2 together through the **back** legs as described in row 1, knit 2* repeat from * to * until the end of the row.

Row 4: Purl all the stitches.

Row 5: *Knit 1, knit 2 together through the **front** legs as described in row 1, knit 1, yarn over forward (i.e., from yourself), knit 5, yarn over forward (i.e., from yourself), knit 1, knit 2 together through the **back** legs as described in row 1, knit 1* repeat from * to * until the end of the row.

Row 6: Purl all the stitches.

Row 7: *Knit 2 together through the **front** legs as described in row 1, knit 1, yarn over forward (i.e., from yourself), knit 7, yarn over forward (i.e., from yourself), knit 1, knit 2 together through the **back** legs as described in row 1* repeat from * to * until the end of the row.

Row 8: Purl all the stitches.

Repeat rows: 1-8.

Bind off after the last row 8 as follows: Slip the edge stitch onto the right needle, knit the next 1, then insert the left needle through the slipped edge stitch, from left to right, and pass it over the knitted stitch, *now there is 1 stitch on the right needle, knit the next 1 (now there are 2 stitches on the right needle), insert the left needle through the 1st stitch on the right needle, from left to right, and pass it over the 2nd one* repeat from * to * until the end of the row.

Pattern 44

Cast on a multiple of 18, plus 3 and 2 edge stitches. Eighteen-stitch repeat. Repeat rows: 1-8. **The edge stitches are not included in the description below and must be added. Slip the first edge stitch, purl the last one.**

Knit through the back leg, purl as follows: with the working yarn in front of the stitch, insert the right needle through the stitch from back to front, move the working yarn under the right needle and pull it with the needle through the stitch. The purl stitch that works this way sets up the knit stitch for knitting through the back leg. **Needles: 2.5 mm.**

Description:

Row 1: *Purl 3, knit 3, knit 2 together through the **front** legs as follows: turn the 1st one on the left needle clockwise twice as follows: insert the right needle through the back leg from back to front and slip it onto the right needle, thus moving the back leg to the front, return this stitch onto the left needle, now the back leg becomes the front one, then insert the right needle through the back leg 1 more time and slip the stitch onto the right needle, thus moving the back leg to the front 1 more time, leave this stitch on the right needle, insert the right needle through the back leg of the 2nd stitch from back to front and slip it onto the right needle, thus moving the back leg to the front, return both stitches onto the left needle, now knit 2 together through the **front** legs, knit 2, yarn over forward (i.e., from yourself), purl 1, yarn over forward (i.e., from yourself), knit 2, knit 2 together through the **back** legs as follows: slip the 1st stitch onto the right needle, turn the 2nd one on the left needle clockwise twice as follows: insert the right needle through the back leg from back to front and slip it onto the right needle, thus moving the back leg to the front, return this stitch onto the left needle, now the back leg becomes the front one, then insert the right needle through the back leg 1 more time and it onto the right needle, thus moving the back leg to the front 1 more time, return this stitch onto the left needle, then return the 1st stitch onto the left one, now knit 2 together through the **back** legs, knit 3* repeat from * to * until the end of the row before the edge stitch purl 3.

Row 2: *Knit 3, purl 7, knit 1, purl 7* repeat from * to * until the end of the row before the edge stitch, knit 3.

Row 3: *Purl 3, knit 2, knit 2 together through the **front** legs as described in row 1, knit 2, yarn over forward (i.e., from yourself), knit 1, purl 1, knit 1, yarn over forward (i.e., from yourself), knit 2, knit 2 together through the **back** legs as described in row 1, knit 2* repeat from * to * until the end of the row before the edge stitch, purl 3.

Row 4: *Knit 3, purl 7, knit 1, purl 7* repeat from * to * until the end of the row before the edge stitch, knit 3.

Row 5: *Purl 3, knit 1, knit 2 together through the **front** legs as described in row 1, knit 2, yarn over forward (i.e., from yourself), knit 2, purl 1, knit 2, yarn over forward (i.e., from yourself), knit 2, knit 2 together through the **back** legs as described in row 1, knit 1* repeat from * to * until the end of the row before the edge stitch, purl 3.

Row 6: *Knit 3, purl 7, knit 1, purl 7* repeat from * to * until the end of the row before the edge stitch, knit 3.

Row 7: *Purl 3, knit 2 together through the **front** legs as described in row 1, knit 2, yarn over forward (i.e., from yourself), knit 3, purl 1, knit 3, yarn over forward (i.e., from yourself), knit 2, knit 2 together through the **back** legs as described in row 1* repeat from * to * until the end of the row before the edge stitch, purl 3.

Row 8: *Knit 3, purl 7, knit 1, purl 7* repeat from * to * until the end of the row before the edge stitch, knit 3.

Repeat rows: 1-8.

Bind off after the last row 8 as follows: Slip the edge stitch onto the right needle, knit the next 1, then insert the left needle through the slipped edge stitch, from left to right, and pass it over the knitted stitch, *now there is 1 stitch on the right needle, knit the next 1 (now there are 2 stitches on the right needle), insert the left needle through the 1st stitch on the right needle, from left to right, and pass it over the 2nd one* repeat from * to * until the end of the row.

Pattern 45

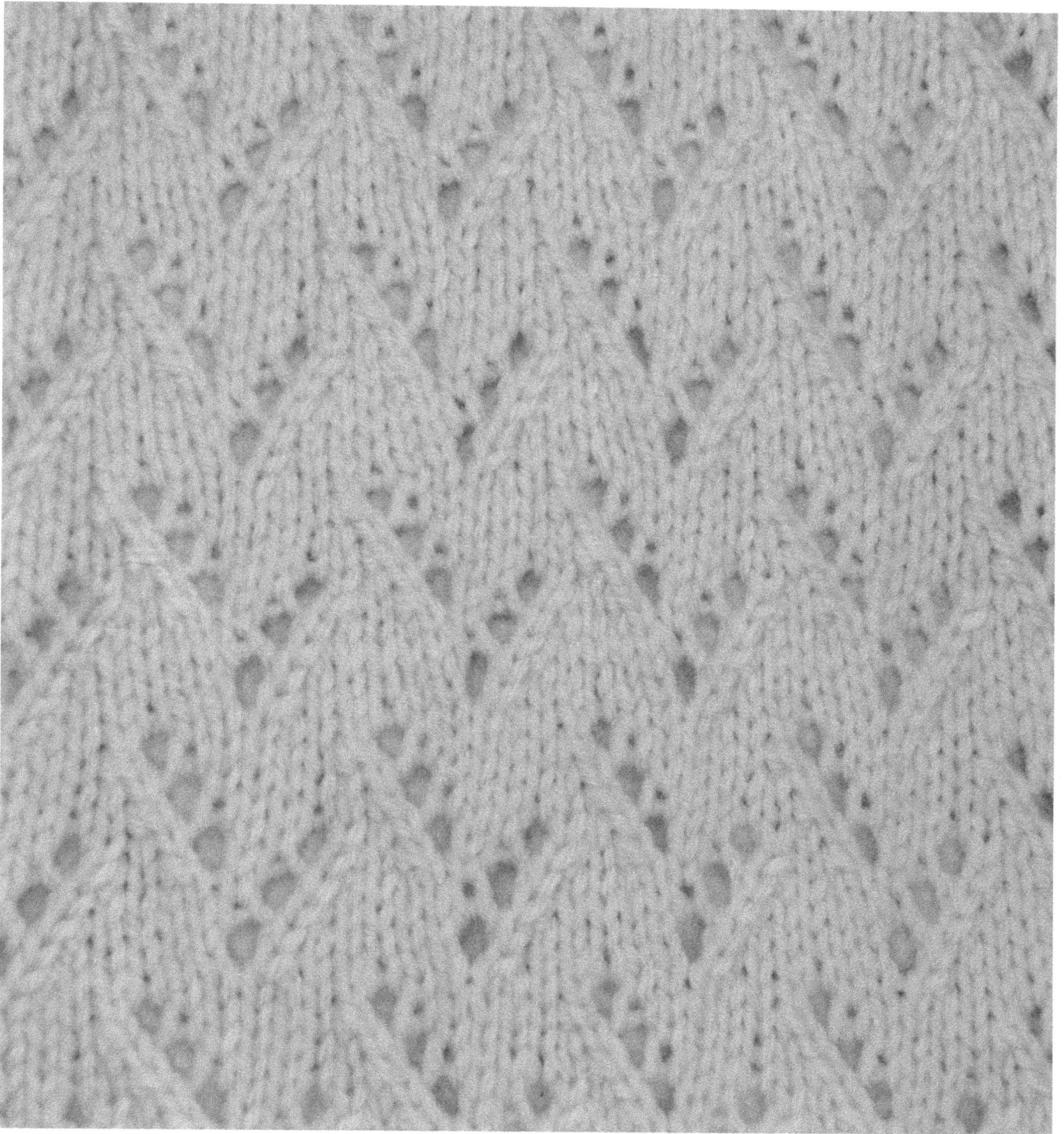

Cast on a multiple of 7, plus 2 edge stitches. Seven-stitch repeat. Repeat rows: 1-10. **The edge stitches are not included in the description below and must be added. Slip the first edge stitch, purl the last one.**

Knit through the back leg, purl as follows: with the working yarn in front of the stitch, insert the right needle through the stitch from back to front, move the working yarn under the right needle and pull it with the needle through the stitch. The purl stitch that works this way sets up the knit stitch for knitting through the back leg. **Needles: 2.5 mm.**

Description:

Row 1: *Knit 5, knit 2 together through the **front** legs as follows: turn the 1st one on the left needle clockwise twice as follows: insert the right needle through the back leg from back to front and slip it onto the right needle, thus moving the back leg to the front, return this stitch onto the left needle, now the back leg becomes the front one, then insert the right needle through the back leg 1 more time and slip it onto the right needle, thus moving the back leg to the front 1 more time, leave this stitch on the right needle, insert the right needle through the back leg of the 2nd stitch from back to front and slip it onto the right needle, thus moving the back leg to the front, return both stitches onto the left needle, now knit 2 together through the **front** legs, then yarn over forward (i.e., from yourself)* repeat from * to * until the end of the row.

Row 2: Purl all the stitches.

Row 3: Knit 4, knit 2 together through the **front** legs as described in row 1, yarn over forward (i.e., from yourself), knit 1* repeat from * to * until the end of the row.

Row 4: Purl all the stitches.

Row 5: *Yarn over forward (i.e., from yourself), knit 2 together through the **back** legs as follows: slip the 1st stitch onto the right needle, turn the 2nd one clockwise twice as follows: insert the right needle through the back leg from back to front and slip it onto the right needle, thus moving the back leg to the front, return this stitch onto the left needle, now the back leg becomes the front one, then insert the right needle through the back leg 1 more time and slip it onto the right needle, thus moving the back leg to the front 1 more time, return this stitch onto the left needle, then return the 1st stitch from the right needle to the left one, now knit 2 together through the back legs, knit 1, knit 2 together through the **front** legs as described in row 1, yarn over forward (i.e., from yourself), knit 2* repeat from * to * until the end of the row.

Row 6: Purl all the stitches.

Row 7: *Knit 1, yarn over forward (i.e., from yourself), knit 2 together through the **back** legs as described in row 1, knit 4* repeat from * to * until the end of the row.

Row 8: Purl all the stitches.

Row 9: *Knit 2, yarn over forward (i.e., from yourself), knit 2 together through the **back** legs as described in row 1, knit 3* repeat from * to * until the end of the row.

Row 10: *Purl all the stitches.

Repeat rows: 1-10.

Bind off after the last row 10 as follows: Slip the edge stitch onto the right needle, knit the next 1, then insert the left needle through the slipped edge stitch, from left to right, and pass it over the knitted stitch, *now there is 1 stitch on the right needle, knit the next 1 (now there are 2 stitches on the right needle), insert the left needle through the 1st stitch on the right needle, from left to right, and pass it over the 2nd one* repeat from * to * until the end of the row.

Pattern 46

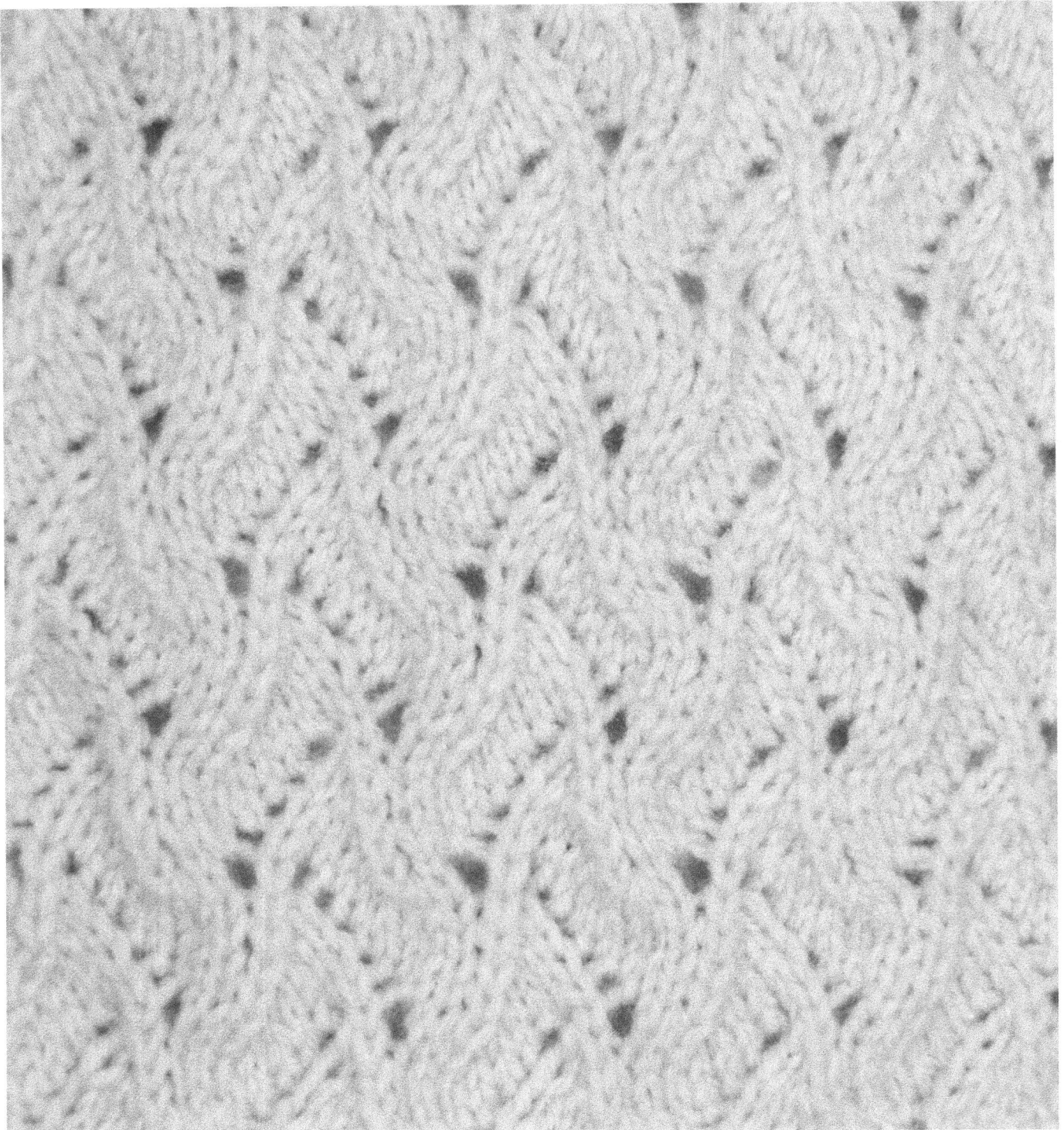

Cast on a multiple of 8 and 2 edge stitches. Eight-stitch repeat. Repeat rows: 1-12. **The edge stitches are not included in the description below and must be added. Slip the first edge stitch, purl the last one.**

Knit through the back leg, purl as follows: with the working yarn in front of the stitch, insert the right needle through the stitch from back to front, move the working yarn under the right needle and pull it with the needle through the stitch. The purl stitch that works this way sets up the knit stitch for knitting through the back leg. **Needles: 2.5 mm.**

Description:

Row 1: *Knit 1, knit 2 together through the **back** legs as follows: slip the 1st stitch onto the right needle, turn the next 1 on the left needle clockwise twice as follows: insert the right needle through the back leg from back to front and slip it onto the right needle, thus moving the back leg to the front, return this stitch onto the left needle, now the back leg becomes the front one, then insert the right needle through the back leg 1 more time and slip it onto the right needle, thus moving the back leg to the front 1 more time, return this stitch onto the left needle, then return the 1st stitch from the right needle to the left one, now knit 2 together through the **back** legs, knit 5, yarn over forward (i.e., from yourself)* repeat from * to * until the end of the row.

Row 2: *Purl 1, yarn over forward (i.e., from yourself), purl 4, purl the next 2 together as follows, to receive the stitch on the front side with a slant to the left: insert the right needle through the back legs of these 2 stitches simultaneously from left to right and slip both stitches onto the right needle, thus moving the back legs to the front, return both stitches onto the left needle, now purl 2 together through the front legs, purl 1* repeat from * to * until the end of the row.

Row 3: *Knit 1, knit 2 together through the **back** legs as described in row 1, knit 3, yarn over forward (i.e., from yourself), knit 2* repeat from * to * until the end of the row.

Row 4: *Purl 3, yarn over forward (i.e., from yourself), purl 2, purl 2 together as described in row 2, to receive the stitch on the front side with a slant to the left, purl 1* repeat from * to * until the end of the row.

Row 5: *Knit 1, knit 2 together through the **back** legs as described in row 1, knit 1, yarn over forward (i.e., from yourself), knit 4* repeat from * to * until the end of the row.

Row 6: *Purl 5, yarn over forward (i.e., from yourself), purl the next 2 together as described in row 2, to receive the stitch on the front side with a slant to the left, purl 1* repeat from * to * until the end of the row.

Row 7: *Knit 1, yarn over forward (i.e., from yourself), knit 5, knit 2 together through the **front** legs as follows: turn the 1st one on the left needle clockwise twice as follows: insert the right needle through the back leg from back to front and slip it onto the right needle, thus moving the back leg to the front, return this stitch onto the left needle, now the back leg becomes the front one, then insert the right needle through the back leg 1 more time and slip it onto the right needle, thus moving the back leg to the front 1 more time, leave this stitch on the right needle, insert the right needle through the back leg of the 2nd stitch from back to front and slip it onto the right needle, thus moving the back leg to the front, return both stitches from the right needle to the left one, now knit 2 together through the **front** legs* repeat from * to * until the end of the row.

Row 8: *Purl 2 together, purl 4, yarn over forward (i.e., from yourself), purl 2* repeat from * to * until the end of the row.

Row 9: *Knit 3, yarn over forward (i.e., to yourself), knit 3, knit 2 together through the **front** legs as described in row 7* repeat from * to * until the end of the row.

Row 10: *Purl 2 together, purl 2, yarn over forward (i.e., from yourself), purl 4* repeat from * to * until the end of the row.

Row 11: *Knit 5, yarn over forward (i.e., to yourself), knit 1, knit 2 together through the **front** legs as described in row 7* repeat from * to * until the end of the row.

Row 12: *Purl 2 together, yarn over forward (i.e., from yourself), purl 6* repeat from * to * until the end of the row.

Repeat rows: 1-12.

Bind off after the last row 12 as follows: Slip the edge stitch onto the right needle, knit the next 1, then insert the left needle through the slipped edge stitch, from left to right, and pass it over the knitted stitch, *now there is 1 stitch on the right needle, knit the next 1 (now there are 2 stitches on the right needle), insert the left needle through the 1st stitch on the right needle, from left to right, and pass it over the 2nd one* repeat from * to * until the end of the row.

Pattern 47

Cast on a multiple of 12 and 2 edge stitches. Twelve-stitch repeat. Repeat rows: 1-8. **The edge stitches are not included in the description below and must be added. Slip the first edge stitch, purl the last one.**

Knit through the back leg, purl as follows: with the working yarn in front of the stitch, insert the right needle through the stitch from back to front, move the working yarn under the right needle and pull it with the needle through the stitch. The purl stitch that works this way sets up the knit stitch for knitting through the back leg. **Needles: 2 mm or 2.5 mm.**

Description:

Row 1: *Knit 1, yarn over forward (i.e., from yourself), knit 3, knit 2 together through the **front** legs as follows: turn the 1st one on the left needle clockwise twice as follows: insert the right needle through the back leg from back to front and slip it onto the right needle, thus moving the back leg to the front, return this stitch onto the left needle, now the back leg becomes the front one, then insert the right needle through the back leg 1 more time and slip the stitch onto the right needle, thus moving the back leg to the front 1 more time, leave this stitch on the right needle, insert the right needle through the back leg of the 2nd stitch from back to front and slip it onto the right needle, thus moving the back leg to the front, return both stitches from onto the left needle, now knit 2 together through the **front** legs, knit 1, knit 2 together through the **back** legs as follows: slip the 1st stitch onto the right needle, turn the 2nd one clockwise twice as follows: insert the right needle through the back leg from back to front and slip it onto the right needle, thus moving the back leg to the front, return this stitch onto the left needle, now the back leg becomes the front one, then insert the right needle through the back leg 1 more time and slip the stitch onto the right needle, thus moving the back leg to the front 1 more time, return this stitch onto the left needle, then return the 1st stitch from the right needle to the left one, now knit 2 together through the **back** legs, knit 3, yarn over forward (i.e., from yourself)* repeat from * to * until the end of the row.

Row 2: *Purl 1, yarn over forward (i.e., from yourself), purl 2, purl the next 2 together as follows (to receive to the stitch on the front side with a slant to the left): insert the right needle through the back legs of these 2 stitches simultaneously from left to right and slip both stitches onto the right needle, thus moving the back legs to the front, return both stitches onto the left needle, now purl 2 together through the front legs, purl 1, purl 2 together, purl 2, yarn over forward (i.e., from yourself), purl 2* repeat from * to * until the end of the row.

Row 3: *Knit 3, yarn over forward (i.e., from yourself), knit 1, knit 2 together through the **front** legs as described in row 1, knit 1, knit 2 together through the **back** legs as described in row 1, knit 1, yarn over forward (i.e., from yourself), knit 2* repeat from * to * until the end of the row.

Row 4: *Purl 3, yarn over forward (i.e., from yourself), purl 2 together as described in row 2, in order to receive the stitch on the front side with a slant to the left, purl 1, purl 2 together, yarn over forward (i.e., from yourself), purl 4* repeat from * to * until the end of the row.

Row 5: *Knit 1, knit 2 together through the **back** legs as described in row 1, knit 3, yarn over forward (i.e., from yourself), knit 1, yarn over forward (i.e., from yourself), knit 3, knit 2 together through the **front** legs as described in row 1* repeat from * to * until the end of the row.

Row 6: *Purl 2 together, purl 2, yarn over forward (i.e., from yourself), purl 3, yarn over forward (i.e., from yourself), purl 2, purl the next 2 together with a slant to the left as described in row 2, purl 1* repeat from * to * until the end of the row.

Row 7: *Knit 1, knit 2 together through the **back** legs as described in row 1, knit 1, yarn over forward (i.e., from yourself), knit 5, yarn over forward (i.e., from yourself), knit 1, knit 2 together through the **front** legs as described in row 1* repeat from * to * until the end of the row.

Row 8: *Purl 2 together, yarn over forward (i.e., from yourself), purl 7, yarn over forward (i.e., from yourself), purl the next 2 together with a slant to the left as described in row 2, purl 1* repeat from * to * until the end of the row.

Repeat rows: 1-8.

Bind off after the last row 8 as follows: Slip the edge stitch onto the right needle, knit the next 1, then insert the left needle through the slipped edge stitch, from left to right, and pass it over the knitted stitch, *now there is 1 stitch on the right needle, knit the next 1 (now there are 2 stitches on the right needle), insert the left needle through the 1st stitch on the right needle, from left to right, and pass it over the 2nd one* repeat from * to * until the end of the row.

Pattern 48

Cast on a multiple of 17, plus 1 for symmetry and 2 edge stitches. Seventeen-stitch repeat. Repeat rows: 1-16. **The edge stitches are not included in the description below and must be added. Slip the first edge stitch, purl the last one.**

Knit through the back leg, purl as follows: with the working yarn in front of the stitch, insert the right needle through the stitch from back to front, move the working yarn under the right needle and pull it with the needle through the stitch. The purl stitch that works this way sets up the knit stitch for knitting through the back leg. **Needles: 2.5 mm.**

Description:

Row 1: *Purl 1, knit 2 together through the **back** legs as follows: slip the 1st stitch onto the right needle, turn the 2nd one clockwise twice as follows: insert the right needle through the back leg from back to front and slip it onto the right needle, thus moving the back leg to the front, return this stitch onto the left needle, now the back leg becomes the front one, then insert the right needle through the back leg 1 more time and slip the stitch onto the right needle, thus moving the back leg to the front 1 more time, return this stitch onto the left needle, then return the 1st stitch onto the left needle, now knit 2 together through the **back** legs, yarn over forward (i.e., from yourself), knit 8, yarn over forward (i.e., from yourself), knit 4, knit 2 together through the **front** legs as follows: turn the 1st one clockwise twice as follows: insert the right needle through the back leg from back to front and slip it onto the right needle, thus moving the back leg to the front, return this stitch onto the left needle, now the back leg becomes the front one, then insert the right needle through the back leg 1 more time and slip the stitch onto the right needle, thus moving the back leg to the front 1 more time, leave this stitch on the right needle, insert the right needle through the back leg of the 2nd stitch from back to front and slip it onto the right needle, thus moving the back leg to the front, return both stitches onto the left needle, now knit 2 together through the **front** legs* repeat from * to * until the end of the row before the edge stitch, purl 1.

Row 2: *Knit 1, purl 16* repeat from * to * until the end of the row before the edge stitch, knit 1.

Row 3: *Purl 1, with the working yarn behind your work slip 4 onto a cable needle behind your work, knit the next 4, then knit the slipped 4, knit 3, yarn over forward (i.e., from yourself), knit 3, knit 2 together through the **front** legs as described in row 1* repeat from * to * until the end of the row before the edge stitch, purl 1.

Row 4: *Knit 1, purl 16* repeat from * to * until the end of the row before the edge stitch, knit 1.

Row 5: *Purl 1, knit 2 together through the **back** legs as described in row 1, knit 6, yarn over forward (i.e., from yourself), knit 4, yarn over forward (i.e., from yourself), knit 2, knit 2 together through the **front** legs as described in row 1* repeat from * to * until the end of the row before the edge stitch, purl 1.

Row 6: *Knit 1, purl 16* repeat from * to * until the end of the row before the edge stitch, knit 1.

Row 7: *Purl 1, knit 2 together through the **back** legs as described in row 1, knit 5, yarn over forward (i.e., from yourself), knit 6, yarn over forward (i.e., from yourself), knit 1, knit 2 together through the **front** legs as described in row 1* repeat from * to * until the end of the row before the edge stitch, purl 1.

Row 8: *Knit 1, purl 16* repeat from * to * until the end of the row before the edge stitch, knit 1.

Row 9: *Purl 1, knit 2 together through the **back** legs as described in row 1, knit 4, yarn over forward (i.e., from yourself), knit 8, yarn over forward (i.e., from yourself), knit 2 together through the **front** legs as described in row 1* repeat from * to * until the end of the row before the edge stitch, purl 1.

Row 10: *Knit 1, purl 16* repeat from * to * until the end of the row before the edge stitch, knit 1.

Row 11: *Purl 1, knit 2 together through the **back** legs as described in row 1, knit 3, yarn over forward (i.e., from yourself), knit 3, slip 4 onto a cable needle in front of your work, knit the next 4, then knit the slipped 4* repeat from * to * until the end of the row before the edge stitch, purl 1.

Row 12: *Knit 1, purl 16* repeat from * to * until the end of the row before the edge stitch, knit 1.

Row 13: *Purl 1, knit 2 together through the **back** legs as described in row 1, knit 2, yarn over forward (i.e., from yourself), knit 4, yarn over forward (i.e., from yourself), knit 6, knit 2 together through the **front** legs as described in row 1* repeat from * to * until the end of the row before the edge stitch, purl 1.

Row 14: *Knit 1, purl 16* repeat from * to * until the end of the row before the edge stitch, knit 1.

Row 15: *Purl 1, knit 2 together through the **back** legs as described in row 1, knit 1, yarn over forward (i.e., from yourself), knit 6, yarn over forward (i.e., from yourself), knit 5, knit 2 together through the **front** legs as described in row 1* repeat from * to * until the end of the row before the edge stitch, purl 1.

Row 16: *Knit 1, purl 16* repeat from * to * until the end of the row before the edge stitch, knit 1.

Repeat rows: 1-16.

Bind off after the last row 16 as follows: Slip the edge stitch onto the right needle, knit the next 1, then insert the left needle through the slipped edge stitch, from left to right, and pass it over the knitted stitch, *now there is 1 stitch on the right needle, knit the next 1 (now there are 2 stitches on the right needle), insert the left needle through the 1st stitch on the right needle, from left to right, and pass it over the 2nd one* repeat from * to * until the end of the row.

Pattern 49

Cast on a multiple of 17, plus 2 edge stitches. Seventeen-stitch repeat. Repeat rows: 1-8. **The edge stitches are not included in the description below and must be added. Slip the first edge stitch, purl the last one.**

Knit through the back leg, purl as follows: with the working yarn in front of the stitch, insert the right needle through the stitch from back to front, move the working yarn under the right needle and pull it with the needle through the stitch. The purl stitch that works this way sets up the knit stitch for knitting through the back leg. **Needles: 2.5 mm.**

Description:

Row 1: *Knit 3, knit 2 together through the **front** legs as follows: turn the 1st one on the left needle clockwise twice as follows: insert the right needle through the back leg from back to front and slip it onto the right needle, thus moving the back leg to the front, return this stitch onto the left needle, now the back leg becomes the front one, then insert the right needle through the back leg 1 more time and slip the stitch onto the right needle, thus moving the back leg to the front 1 more time, leave this stitch on the right needle, insert the right needle through the back leg of the 2nd stitch from back to front and slip it onto the right needle, thus moving the back leg to the front, return both stitches onto the left needle, now knit 2 together through the **front** legs,knit 3, yarn over forward (i.e., from yourself), knit 1, yarn over forward (i.e., from yourself), knit 3, knit 2 together through the **back** legs as follows: slip the 1st stitch onto the right needle, turn the 2nd one clockwise twice as follows: insert the right needle through the back leg from back to front and slip it onto the right needle, thus moving the back leg to the front, return this stitch onto the left needle, now the back leg becomes the front one, then insert the right needle through the back leg 1 more time and slip the stitch onto the right needle, thus moving the back leg to the front 1 more time, return this stitch onto the left needle, then return the 1st stitch onto the left one, now knit 2 together through the **back** legs, knit 3* repeat from * to * until the end of the row.

Row 2: Purl all the stitches.

Row 3: *Knit 2, knit 2 together through the **front** legs as described in row 1, knit 3, yarn over forward (i.e., from yourself), knit 3, yarn over forward (i.e., from yourself), knit 3, knit 2 together through the **back** legs as described in row 1, knit 2* repeat from * to * until the end of the row.

Row 4: Purl all the stitches.

Row 5: *Knit 1, knit 2 together through the **front** legs as described in row 1, knit 3, yarn over forward (i.e., from yourself), knit 5, yarn over forward (i.e., from yourself), knit 3, knit 2 together through the **back** legs as described in row 1, knit 1* repeat from * to * until the end of the row.

Row 6: Purl all the stitches.

Row 7: *Knit 2 together through the **front** legs as described in row 1, knit 3, yarn over forward (i.e., from yourself), knit 7, yarn over forward (i.e., from yourself), knit 3, knit 2 together through the **back** legs as described in row 1* repeat from * to * until the end of the row.

Row 8: Purl all the stitches.

Repeat rows: 1-8.

Bind off after the last row 8 as follows: Slip the edge stitch onto the right needle, knit the next 1, then insert the left needle through the slipped edge stitch, from left to right, and pass it over the knitted stitch, *now there is 1 stitch on the right needle, knit the next 1 (now there are 2 stitches on the right needle), insert the left needle through the 1st stitch on the right needle, from left to right, and pass it over the 2nd one* repeat from * to * until the end of the row.

Pattern 50

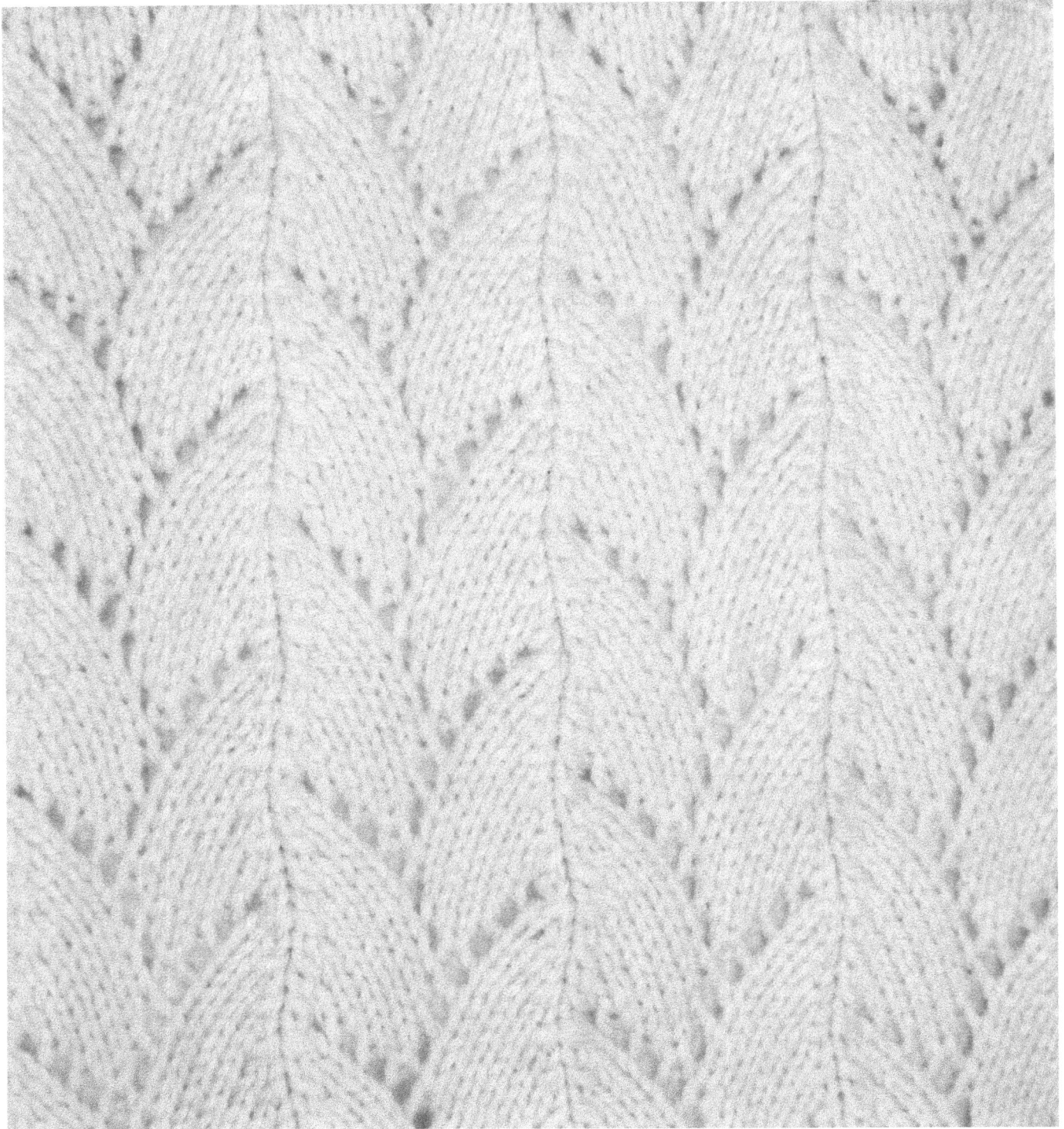

Cast on a multiple of 12 and 2 edge stitches. Twelve-stitch repeat. Repeat rows: 1-12. **The edge stitches are not included in the description below and must be added. Slip the first edge stitch, purl the last one.**

Knit through the back leg, purl as follows: with the working yarn in front of the stitch, insert the right needle through the stitch from back to front, move the working yarn under the right needle and pull it with the needle through the stitch. The purl stitch that works this way sets up the knit stitch for knitting through the back leg. **Needles: 2.5 mm.**

Description:

Row 1: *Knit 2 together through the **front** legs as follows: slip the 1st stitch onto the right needle, inserting the right needle through the back leg from back to front, thus moving the back leg to the front, slip the 2nd stitch onto the right needle as follows: insert the right needle through the back leg from back to front, thus moving the back leg of the 2nd stitch to the front, return both stitches onto the left needle, now knit 2 together through the **front** legs, then knit 2, yarn over forward (i.e., from yourself), knit 1, yarn over forward (i.e., from yourself), knit 5, knit 2 together through the **back** legs* repeat from * to * until the end of the row.

Row 2: Purl all the stitches.

Row 3: *Knit 2 together through the **front** legs as described in row 1, knit 1, yarn over forward (i.e., from yourself), knit 3, yarn over forward (i.e., from yourself), knit 4, knit 2 together through the **back** legs* repeat from * to * until the end of the row.

Row 4: *Purl all the stitches.

Row 5: *Knit 2 together through the **front** legs as described in row 1, yarn over forward (i.e., from yourself), knit 5, yarn over forward (i.e., from yourself), knit 3, knit 2 together through the **back** legs* repeat from * to * until the end of the row.

Row 6: Purl all the stitches.

Row 7: *Knit 2 together through the **front** legs as described in row 1, knit 5, yarn over forward (i.e., from yourself), knit 1, yarn over forward (i.e., from yourself), knit 2, knit 2 together through the **back** legs* repeat from * to * until the end of the row.

Row 8: Purl all the stitches.

Row 9: *Knit 2 together through the **front** legs as described in row 1, knit 4, yarn over forward (i.e., from yourself), knit 3, yarn over forward (i.e., from yourself), knit 1, knit 2 together through the **back** legs* repeat from * to * until the end of the row.

Row 10: Purl all the stitches.

Row 11: *Knit 2 together through the **front** legs as described in row 1, knit 3, yarn over forward (i.e., from yourself), knit 5, yarn over forward (i.e., from yourself), knit 2 together through the **back** legs* repeat from * to * until the end of the row.

Row 12: Purl all the stitches.

Repeat rows: 1-12.

Bind off after the last row 12 as follows: Slip the edge stitch onto the right needle, knit the next 1, then insert the left needle through the slipped edge stitch, from left to right, and pass it over the knitted stitch, *now there is 1 stitch on the right needle, knit the next 1 (now there are 2 stitches on the right needle), insert the left needle through the 1st stitch on the right needle, from left to right, and pass it over the 2nd one* repeat from * to * until the end of the row.

About The Author

Internationally recognized hand knitwear designer Marina Molo has taught on various aspects of hand knitting over the past 30 years. In her book, 50 Shades of Stitches Vol. 5, Marina Molo brings to life, in print, the most popular knitting patterns, Braids & Cables, for all those who want to explore designing their knitwear.

Visit the author's online store for unique items with knit prints, which include tank tops, leggings, tote bags, iPhone cases, passport holders, luggage tags, wrapping paper, ribbons, pattern folders & much more at https://www.zazzle.com/store/shades_of_stitches_or scan QR:

Marina Molo is currently working on several new publishing projects with SCR Media Inc.

Sign up to be notified when the next release is available at **www.MarinaMolo.com**.

What Do You Think of 50 Shades of Stitches?

First of all, thank you for purchasing this book, *50 Shades of Stitches Volume 5.*

I know you could have chosen any other books to read, but you chose this book, and for that, I am incredibly grateful. I hope that it adds value and quality to your everyday life. If so, it would be nice if you could share this book with your friends and family by posting it on *Facebook* and *Twitter.*

If you like this book and found some benefit in reading it, I'd like to hear from you and hope that you could take some time to post a review on Amazon. Your feedback and support will help the author to improve her writing craft for future projects and make this book even better. Just type this link into your web browser **Getbook.at/Vol5** or scan the code below:

I want you, the reader, to know that your review is important, and so if you'd like to leave a review, all you have to do is copy it into your web browser *Getbook.at/Vol5.*

I wish you all the best in your future success!

www.ingramcontent.com/pod-product-compliance
Lightning Source LLC
Chambersburg PA
CBHW080623030426
42336CB00018B/3062